HAND IN HAND

Hand in Hand

Devotions for the Later- (and Lately-) Married

KAY MARSHALL STROM
and
DANIEL E. KLINE
(a happily married couple)

SERVANT PUBLICATIONS
ANN ARBOR, MICHIGAN

Copyright 2003 by Kay Marshall Strom and Daniel E. Kline
All rights reserved.

Vine Books is an imprint of Servant Publications especially designed to serve evangelical Christians.

Servant Mission Statement

We are dedicated to publishing books that spread the gospel of Jesus Christ, help Christians to live in accordance with that gospel, promote renewal in the church, and bear witness to Christian unity.

Unless otherwise noted, Scripture has been quoted from the HOLY BIBLE, NEW INTERNATIONAL VERSION®. Copyright 1973, 1978, 1984 by International Bible Society. Used by permission of Zondervan Publishing House. All rights reserved. Passages marked KJV are from the King James Version. Passages marked NRSV are from the New Revised Standard Version. Passages marked NKJV are from the New King James Version.

Published by Servant Publications
P.O. Box 8617
Ann Arbor, Michigan 48107
www.servantpub.com

Cover design: Alan Furst, Minneapolis, Minn.

03 04 05 06 10 9 8 7 6 5 4 3 2 1

Printed in the United States of America
ISBN 1-56955-295-9

Library of Congress Cataloging-in-Publication Data

Strom, Kay Marshall, 1943-
  Hand in hand : devotions for the later-- (and lately--) married / Kay Marshall Strom and Daniel E. Kline.
    p. cm.
  ISBN 1-56955-295-9 (alk. paper)
  1. Spouses--Prayer-books and devotions--English. 2. Middle aged persons--Prayer-books and devotions--English. I. Kline, Daniel E., 1944- II. Title.
  BV4596.M3.S767 2003
  242'.644--dc21

2003004772

Dedication

We lovingly dedicate this book to

Marjorie and Albert Marshall,
Kay's parents,
who, as we complete this writing,
are celebrating their sixty-third wedding anniversary,
and to Ed and Grace Kline,
Dan's parents,
who were married sixty years, until death parted them.

Contents

Introduction / 9

1. Love at First Sight? / 11
2. The Hope of Heaven / 13
3. Sisters and Brothers and Cousins and Aunts / 15
4. Adopted and Accepted / 17
5. A Home for Us / 19
6. Two Truths and a Secret / 21
7. Drip, Drip, Drip / 23
8. Got-To's and Get-To's / 25
9. Laboring Hand in Hand / 27
10. Looking to the Hills / 29
11. A Few of Her Favorite Things / 31
12. Never Too Much / 33
13. A Mountaintop Experience / 35
14. An Eternal Gift / 37
15. Honest-Honest? / 39
16. What If ...? / 41
17. Window of Opportunity / 43
18. Wet Neck Syndrome / 45
19. Comfortable as a Slipper / 47
20. Songs in the Dark / 49
21. To Love Again / 51
22. God's Favorites / 53
23. Pray First! / 55
24. Evergreen Lodge / 57
25. Thanks, Mom And Dad! / 59
26. Good Old Days / 61
27. Little Things Count / 63
28. A Day of Trouble / 65

29.	Sanity File	/ 67
30.	A Tongue Under Control	/ 69
31.	The Gift of Forgiveness	/ 71
32.	Time Flies—Or Does It?	/ 73
33.	Well-Aimed Prayer	/ 75
34.	The Sun Is Setting	/ 77
35.	Stop My Tongue!	/ 79
36.	A Hike in the Hills	/ 81
37.	No Competition	/ 83
38.	Ultimate Trust	/ 85
39.	All We Are and All We Have ...	/ 87
40.	"And Yet ..."	/ 89
41.	A Sacrifice of Love	/ 91
42.	Never Too Weak to Give, Never Too Strong to Ask	/ 93
43.	Not Distant Enough	/ 95
44.	The Very Last Word	/ 97
45.	... And The Truth Will Set You Free	/ 99
46.	True Beauty	/ 101
47.	One Gripe Too Many	/ 103
48.	Meaningless?	/ 105
49.	Lesson From a Woman on a Bus	/ 107
50.	Supporting the Family	/ 109
51.	Someone to Depend On	/ 111
52.	Who Is in Control?	/ 113
53.	Generosity of Spirit	/ 115
54.	That They Might Be Won Over	/ 117
55.	No Longer Children	/ 119
56.	Who Is My Neighbor?	/ 121
57.	The Family Flock	/ 123
58.	Faith, Hope ... and God's Limitless Mercy	/ 125
59.	Saying the Hard Things	/ 127
60.	The Greatest of These	/ 129

Introduction

When we were married, we weren't exactly what you would call the picture-perfect blushing young bride and nervous young groom, as you will see when you get to know us in the pages of this book. Rather than charting the beginning of adulthood together, we were concerned with how we were going to manage to get two households of accumulated stuff merged into one place.

Not long after we were married, we happened to glance at a listing of the public records in the newspaper. "Look at the ages listed by the marriage licenses!" Kay exclaimed. "Fully half of them are thirty-five or older—just like us!"

We started to check more closely, not only in our own county but elsewhere in the country as well. Sure enough, there are just about as many of us (more mature newlyweds, that is) as there are of them (the teens and twenties marriage set).

It was out of this discovery that our marriage book *The Savvy Couples' Guide to Marrying After Thirty-Five* was born. For as you have likely discovered, there are some wonderful blessings and joys that come from blending two fully formed lives together in a marriage, but there are also some real adjustments to be made and challenges to be faced. We found that if this blending of lives is to be successful, two things are rock-bottom essentials: spending quality time together as a couple and spending time together considering truths from God's Word. What better way to accomplish both of these than to set aside time each day to read a devotional prepared specifically for us married-laters? It is our prayer that each meditation will be a springboard for your own discussion of how you might apply that day's principle from God's Word to your own lives and relationship.

We consider it a privilege to share our lives with you. Now we invite you to step away from your busy lives and spend some time together in the presence of the Lord.

ONE

Love at First Sight?

A wife of noble character who can find? She is worth far more than rubies.... She brings him good, not harm, all the days of her life.

Proverbs 31:10-12

I'll never forget the first time I laid eyes on Susan. It was February, I was twenty-two and in college, and it was the beginning of the spring term. Late in that first day of the term I walked into my Spanish 2 class and there she was. Love at first sight.

She was a little over five feet tall, with a slender, graceful figure, gorgeous legs, and a pixie-cap of thick, dark brown hair. Yet her most stunning feature was her eyes—large and brilliant, with a unique and captivating light blue-green color. She was beautiful. She was wonderful. She was the teaching assistant. Uh-oh.

I worked hard, made straight A's, and waited until the semester ended to ask her out: on the last page of the final (I aced it), I wrote—in Spanish—"Would you like to go with me to the movies this weekend?" She accepted. We dated for about six months, fell in love, and then were married at Christmastime that same year. Impetuous? Maybe. Yet we had a lot in common and enjoyed our twin children and fifteen years of married life together. I'll never know just how a lifetime of marriage would have worked out, however, because she died suddenly at the age of forty-two.

By now I was hooked on love and marriage, *and* on the mistaken belief that "true love" equated to "love at first sight." The only other time I had been deeply in love was with my high school sweetheart, and that had started the same way—one look and WHAM! So I thought that was just how it worked.

That's why, a year and a half later, I was not surprised to be married again. Yes, there were some practical reasons, but the biggest reason was simply that I was attracted to her—she had a dazzling smile—and it was another case of love at first sight.

This time we really were impetuous, and unlike Susan and I, my second wife and I had little in common. That seemed great at first, but the differences between us were too much for the relationship to bear, and our too-hasty rush to the altar ended in divorce four years later.

I was then single for ten years, during which time I met Kay. Although I have always found Kay attractive, this was *not* a case of love at first sight. I made sure of that. I was determined not to make the same impetuous mistakes again. But then I worried, *Isn't love supposed to be about the heart and not the head? Am I being cold and calculating in weighing all the pros and cons so carefully?* My problem became one of trying to balance the passion of the heart with the logic of the head. Not an easy task, but one well worth the effort.

Well, over the years we went from casual acquaintances to friends to business associates to close friends until, eventually, we realized we'd fallen in love and *then* we decided to marry. It's been a long time in coming but certainly worth the wait. I now have the honor of being married to not only the person I love most, but the person I respect and admire most as well. What about love at first sight? Yes, it sounds very romantic, but it shouldn't be the only basis on which to build a lifetime relationship.

Prayer:
Lord, please give me wisdom and patience
to temper my passionate heart.

TWO

The Hope of Heaven

My flesh and my heart may fail, but God is the strength of my heart and my portion forever.

PSALM 73:26

Both Dan and I have painfully witnessed firsthand just how weak the human body can be. Dan's first wife, Susan, was only forty-one when she went to the doctor to find the source of the discomfort in her abdomen and found she was riddled with untreatable cancer. She died four months later, leaving Dan in shock and grief to raise twelve-year-old twins alone.

My first husband Larry's illness from a genetic condition lasted much longer and was more drawn out, but after slowly robbing him of his ability to reason and the use of much of his body, it also took his life at far too young an age.

Because of our difficult past experiences, and because we married at an older age, we can't help but ponder just what our time together will eventually bring. Each of us can't help but wonder:

Will I one day be called upon to be caregiver for another terminally ill spouse?
Will my spouse one day have to nurse me though such an illness?
Could either of us bear to put the other through that again?
Would either of us have the strength to go through it again?

None of us can see the future ... and for that we are thankful indeed!

When Larry's condition grew too difficult for me to handle at home, I had to move him into a care facility. I spent time with him there every day, and so got to know several of the other residents. One special lady was Earlene, a dear Christian woman in her sixties who had been in the facility for seven years, ever since she'd had a stroke during surgery.

One time I foolishly and thoughtlessly said, "Oh, Earlene, it must be so frustrating for you to be in here. What a waste of your life!"

Earlene answered, "Oh, no! In here, I work for the Lord, and the Lord works on me!"

That's exactly what we want for ourselves. Right here and now, while we are healthy and capable of actively going about our Father's business. We want lives molded and refined by the Lord.

One day our flesh will fail us. How it will happen, or to which one first, we have no way of knowing. Yet this we do know: We want to make the most of the time allotted us. Furthermore, of this we are assured: God will be our portion for all eternity, for our hope is the hope of heaven.

Prayer:
Eternal Father, be our strength today
and our portion forevermore. May we crave
no other assurance than this.

THREE

Sisters and Brothers and Cousins and Aunts

Carry each other's burdens, and in this way you will fulfill the law of Christ.

GALATIANS 6:1

It was just after Christmas and Dan and I were spending the day at Dan's sister Suzie's house. The living room was brightly decorated and her tree so loaded with ornaments—many large and ornate—that I could hardly see the branches. Each ornament was different, each one unique, and Suzie could tell me where she got each one and when.

Suzie loves Christmas. She also loves puzzles. We got her one of the Grand Canyon, the intricate puzzle sealed in a bottle. It was one of three puzzles she received. Anyone who really knows Suzie knows she can't have too many new puzzles, and the more challenging and ... well, impossible-looking, the better.

Suzie may be ten years older than I. Her politics may be different. There may be few similarities in our lives. Yet it is important to me to spend time with her and to really get to know her because she has been such a vitally important part of Dan's life. She helped to make him who he is today.

"But I'm not marrying the family!" some people (maybe even you?) insist. Wrong! When you married your spouse, you *did* marry the family. That dear one sitting next to you *is* the family. The brothers and sisters, the mom and the dad, the aunts and uncles and cousins—to one degree or another, they are all a part of the person you married.

As is usual whenever Dan and I are with Suzie, one of the things I most enjoyed during this last visit was listening to her stories about the days when Dan was just little Danny, getting into all kinds of mischief. As I listened to her talk, I glanced from older sister to younger brother, and I could see the strong bond of caring that still exists between the two of them.

Before we all said good-bye, I touched Suzie's arm and took her aside to tell her how much I appreciate and love her. I tried to convey to her how very dear she is to me because of all she has meant and still means to Dan, but I'm afraid my words didn't do my feelings justice. My mouth just could not form the words that were so perfectly clear in my heart.

You know what? Just a month earlier, as we left my parents' house, out of the corner of my eye I caught a glimpse of Dan hugging my sister Jo Jeanne. I have a feeling he was saying the very same things to her.

Is there anyone in your expanded family who needs an extra word of appreciation? Today just might be the day to give it.

Prayer:

Thank you, dear Lord, for all the people You have put in both our lives to nurture and protect us. Help us to be faithful in expressing our appreciation to them. May we also show Your love in the way we love each other.

FOUR

Adopted and Accepted

Where you go I will go, and where you stay I will stay. Your people will be my people and your God my God.
RUTH 2:16

I approach my fifty-eighth birthday as an orphan. I don't really feel like an orphan, but technically I am one. My dad died ten years ago at age eighty-six, and shortly after his death my mom moved back to Chicago to live with her twin sister. Eight years later, she and my Aunt Elsie passed away within a few months of each other, both just past ninety-five.

I have nothing to complain about. I grew up in a home with both my parents present, and they were around until I was well into middle age. Besides, it's not unusual for a person my age to be without parents; most of my friends are orphans now, too.

Still, there is a hole somewhere deep inside of me, and it would be all the deeper and more painful if not for my in-laws, who have adopted me as their son and a part of their families. Not actually "adopted"—nothing that formal—but they have taken me into their hearts and made me one of theirs, and it is a wonderful and sustaining feeling.

First there is Margaret, the mother of my first wife, Susan. Back in 1967, when Susan and I were married, both of my parents were alive and very much kicking, so I didn't think of Margaret and my father-in-law Roy as "parents" at that time. But then we lost Susan in 1983 and Roy in 1986, both to cancer. Those of us left drew closer after that. Margaret, as grandmother to our children and great-grandmother to their children, has become the unofficial matriarch of that side of the family.

Now, since 1998, I have Kay's folks, Marjorie and Albert, as my "adoptive" parents in addition to sweet Margaret. I cannot tell you how much they make me feel at home, and they always have, even before Kay and I married. I first met them years ago at their home in Auburn, California, when I stopped by on a business trip from Reno to Davis. They'd never laid eyes on me before, but they welcomed me like a long-lost child.

I'm now convinced that whether by blood, marriage, or some other connection, true family relationships reside in the hearts of those involved. History and Christianity are filled with examples of outsiders adopted into family and faith, and Ruth is a favorite illustration. She was a Moabite, yet she cast her fate completely with Naomi, an Israelite. For all she knew then, she and Naomi would likely die in a land both strange and foreign to her. She had no way of knowing what ultimate plan God had for her, Boaz, and subsequent generations, right down to King David and our Lord Jesus.

Marrying Kay brought me into the family of God's people as well. This Protestantism I've come to believe in, was strange and new to me. It's been a short time—only five or six years—since I accepted Christ as my Savior, but what a change from what I expected! And who but the Lord knows where He is taking us? Where God is leading us we can't see, but we know it is to some valuable work He has set aside for us to do together. Like Ruth, I've put my faith in the Lord and cast my fate with my new family, and I've never felt more loved, accepted, or secure.

Prayer:
Dear Lord, let me be ever worthy of Your promised salvation, an adopted and accepted member of Your family.

FIVE

A Home for Us

The Lord giveth and the Lord taketh away. Blessed be the name of the Lord.

JOB 1:21, KJV

My first husband, Larry, and I were preparing to go on what we called our last family vacation together. Our son Eric had just graduated from high school and our daughter Lisa was already in college. Even this last trip had been hard to arrange. Yet it had been so long in the planning, and was to be so special. We were going to spend two entire weeks in Great Britain!

I was bustling around with a long list of things to get finished before we left when Charles, an attorney for whom I did some editing, called and told me that before we embarked on such a trip, Larry and I should have our wills updated. Oh, and we should also have our house appraised and our insurance checked, he added.

"Yeah, sure," I told him. "I'll put it all on my list of things to do."

I rolled my eyes and went back to more practical things, like planning Eric's graduation buffet and getting Lisa's airline ticket ordered and off to her.

Two days later Charles called again. "Have you taken care of those things yet?" he asked.

"No," I said a bit impatiently, "but I will." Then I promptly moved on to more pressing matters.

Two days later he called again. Then again. Soon he was calling every day. Finally, just to get Charles off my back, I said, "OK! I'll do it today!"

We never did get the wills updated, but I did call the insurance adjuster. Sure enough, our house was way underinsured. It so happened that the insurance company had started offering a replacement package for the house and everything in it for just an extra three dollars a month. I wrote out a check on the spot.

Two days before we were to come home from that last family vacation ever, we were awakened in Oxford, England, by a telephone call from Santa Barbara, California. A wildfire had swept down the mountains and roared through our neighborhood. Our house and everything in it had been destroyed.

How it hurts when the Lord takes away what we never thought we could part with! When our family got back from England, only a pile of ashes and rubble was left where our home had been just weeks before. And the loss didn't end there. Larry's health began a steady decline that ended in his death seven years later at the age of fifty-five.

Dan knows a lot about taking away, too. He never expected to be a widower at thirty-eight with twelve-year-old twins to raise alone.

Oh, but the Lord gives, too. How He gives! He gave Dan and me each other. Instead of just two children each, we have four children between us, and some in-laws and grandchildren to boot. He gave us a fresh relationship with Him and a new church where everyone has known us only together. Oh, yes. And He gave us a home that is truly our own.

Prayer:
Father, grant us gratitude and open hands when You graciously give to us. And when You see fit to take away, give us faith to say, "Blessed be Your name, O Lord!"

SIX

Two Truths and a Secret

There is no fear in love, but perfect love casts out fear.
1 JOHN 4:18, NRSV

A group of us were playing two truths and a lie, a game where each person gives three statements, only two of which are true. Then everyone else tries to guess which statement is the lie. The goal is to try to trick everyone into making the wrong choice. When it was Aaron's turn, he said, "I was bucked off a horse, I spent time in jail, I was married before." Easy, everyone said. Even his new wife Sandy exclaimed, "You were never in jail!"

"Wrong!" he responded. "I was never bucked off a horse."

Sandy's eyes filled with tears. "You mean you really *were* in jail? Why didn't you ever tell me?"

Aaron explained that it had happened when he was in college. He and a couple of other guys had been involved in a graffiti prank and had ended up spending the night in jail. Yet, despite the explanation, Aaron and Sandy left the party early—and they weren't speaking. *If he kept that secret from me, what else is he hiding?* Sandy wondered. *How can I ever trust him again?*

When we come into marriage, we lug along with us twenty, thirty, even forty years of baggage. Some of that is musty laundry. Some may be downright dirty. Certainly there are things we would love to forget.

How forthcoming have you been with each other about your past? Have you talked about the failed college course? The shoplifting arrest? That other person you almost married? The time you ... well, you get the idea.

Perhaps you have come to terms with your own past. You may even feel you have shared everything that needs to be shared with your partner. Or if you haven't, you may feel sure your spouse wouldn't react all that badly if you were to bare your soul. Then again ...

One thing is certain: God knows about every wrong you have ever committed. And unlike the most loving of human beings, His love is unconditional and His forgiveness is infinite.

Your marriage is a new beginning. Don't let the follies of your past hang over you and cloud the present. Confess what you can and what you need to, then turn the rest over to God. If your conscience continues to be burdened by something that, were it to be shared with your spouse, might cause damage to your marriage relationship, search out a professional Christian counselor with whom you can talk it over.

The health of your marriage rests on the mercy of a loving, forgiving God. He can make even the roughest pathways smooth. He can heal even the most grievous wounds from the past.

Prayer:

Father, even when we confess our sins to You and receive Your forgiveness, we may not be able to confess them to each other. Show us what we need to share with each other and what would only cause pain.

SEVEN

Drip, Drip, Drip

The Lord will bless his people with peace.
PSALM 29:11

It was a lazy Saturday morning at the end of a long and tiring week. No kids at home. No place we had to be or jobs that had to be done. Just the two of us sleeping late with the cats snuggled between us. Ahhhh, pure joy. Then I heard it ... drip, drip, drip, drip.

Is there anything more irritating than a dripping faucet? You just drift off to sleep, then ... drip, drip, drip! Finally it isn't even possible to drift off any more. You're too busy anticipating that next drip.

People can irritate in the same way. Yes, even your loving spouse, in his or her own loving way, can be like that dripping faucet.

"Have you mowed the lawn yet? I've had to remind you several times now. It's not getting any cooler outside, you know."

Drip, drip, drip.

"Remember, tonight's your turn to wash the dishes. They're still sitting there."

Drip, drip, drip.

"Where is the tape? Where do we keep the scissors? I need you to get them for me."

Drip, drip, drip.

Whatever it is, for some reason your spouse feels it needs attention *right now*, and just won't let it go. The only way to "stop the drip" is for you to turn off the computer or whatever you're doing and mow the lawn ... now. To stop playing with the kids and wash the dishes ... now. To put down the magazine and personally locate the tape and the scissors ... now. Yes, the job gets done. Yet something else happens, too: Frustration and resentment build up in your spouse. Not because of the task itself, but because it isn't being done willingly or out of love or with a desire to please. No, it is done out of a need to shut off that irritating drip, drip, drip ...

Don't allow irritations over inconsequential things to spoil the happiness and peace that should mark your marriage.

To the irritated spouse: Respond to the drip, drip, drip with a gentle but timely reminder that the job *will* be done. In as kind a way as possible, let your partner know that no more reminders are necessary.

To the offending spouse: Turn off your dripping faucet and give your dear one some peace.

Prayer:

Dear Lord, give us the patience and resolve to resist irritating each other. Help us to respond to one another with peace, patience, and love.

EIGHT

Got-To's and Get-To's

And whatever you do, whether in word or deed, do it all in the name of the Lord Jesus, giving thanks to God the Father through him.

COLOSSIANS 3:17

I make hot cocoa for Kay almost every morning I'm home. Whether I'm home or not, Kay makes the bed most mornings. Although I'm a coffee drinker, I *like* to make the cocoa because it pleases Kay. Kay is not crazy about making the bed alone, but she shows her love for me in the simple act of letting me out of that chore.

Most of the things we do in our lives break down into two simple groups: The things we have to do, and the things we want to do. The first are the "got-to's," the things that can cause resentment, or at the very least are often avoided. The second are the "get-to's," the things that can bring contentment and are often sought out. What is the difference between the two? Nothing more than attitude.

Take, for example, going to work. For many people this falls somewhere between an unpleasant chore and a downright onerous drudge. Yet for others, *doing the exact same work*, it is not only pleasant, it's an honor—it's a gift, a privilege, a ... well, it's a *get-to*.

People who learn to arrive at this state are fortunate. They are happier, healthier, more positive, more balanced, more effective, and certainly more productive. What a great place to be!

The same principle applies to marriage. There are always things you've "got to" do. Here's the trick: whatever it is, as long as you have to do it, why not *pretend*—at least at first—that you see it as a privilege and are happy to do it.

You probably won't be very convincing, even to yourself, especially if this is a real change for you.

How would your spouse react if you were to say, "Honey, I'll be happy to take out the trash right now. Anything else I can do while I'm at it?" Or how about, "Dear, I'll be glad to mend that missing button on your shirt."

Your partner might think you're being sarcastic or otherwise up to something. And you may not really want to do the task at all—at first. Yet, think about it: to keep peace in the family, you have to do it some time or other; it's a got-to. And if you have to do it anyway, the only real choice you have is the degree of grace with which you do it. You can be begrudging, you can procrastinate, you can hope to get out of it somehow. Or, you can do it now—gracefully, willingly, and to the best of your ability.

If we look upon any great or small thing God gives us to do as the privilege it truly is, it becomes a "get-to," an act of Christian love. And it can give enormous satisfaction to the doer as well as to the receiver.

Prayer:

Father, Your supreme command is for us to love and serve You with all we have, and to likewise love others as we do ourselves. Help us to see that we keep both commands, in love and in joy, every time we take advantage of the dozens of daily opportunities You give us to serve each other.

NINE

Laboring Hand in Hand

He has made everything beautiful in its time. He has also set eternity in the hearts of men; they cannot fathom what God has done from beginning to end.
ECCLESIASTES 3:11

Kim and Doug are a young couple who serve on the mission committee at church with us. They spent their honeymoon in Honduras, helping to rebuild a village devastated by a hurricane. Their hearts are dedicated to serving the Lord, and they are not the least bit hesitant to leave the comfort of Santa Barbara if that's what God would have them do. So it was with great excitement that I approached Kim with my latest writing adventure:

"We're going to interview women from the areas most inhospitable to Christianity—China, Indonesia, India, North Africa. Mostly Muslim, but not all. We really need a photographer to travel with us. How about you, Kim? We will be gone for a month, but it will be so worth it! It will fit right in with your talents! It's the chance of a lifetime. How about it?"

Kim would have loved to go. I tried to talk her into going. Yet she stayed home. Why? Because Doug and Kim had made a conscious decision that they would minister together, and this was an opportunity for just Kim.

As a couple who came together with jobs and ministries and possibilities and ideas already intact, Dan and I were taken aback at Doug and Kim's commitment. Building our lives from scratch isn't possible for those of us who come together with so much life behind us. Because Doug and Kim's approach is so distant from the reality of my life, I really don't know whether I would want to do what they are doing, even if I could.

Yet Kim's decision has caused me to think differently about taking such a potentially life-changing journey without Dan. Could he possibly understand the impact of the grinding poverty of low-caste Indian Dalits who have been stripped of their meager possessions simply because they have renounced Hinduism and become Christians? Would he ever be able to understand the fear of discovery I had felt as I hunkered down in an underground church in China?

I followed my own track and went to Asia and India without Dan, and Dan continued with the job to which he was committed. Yet we learned something important from Doug and Kim. Four months later, when it was time for me to conduct the final interviews for the book in North Africa, Dan was there by my side. Months earlier, while I was in China, he had begun adjusting his schedule to make it possible.

We came together with two separate lives running on two separate tracks. Yet we, too, want to minister together.

Prayer:
Help us, Father God, to look to You to show us the right time to walk our own road and when to labor together, hand in hand.

TEN

Looking to the Hills

I lift up my eyes to the hills—where does my help come from? My help comes from the Lord, the Maker of heaven and earth.

PSALM 121:1-2

We have been gifted with access to a very special retreat nestled in the mountains, a place made accessible to only a few select people. When the constantly ringing telephone and the beckoning computers and the nagging piles of work to be done get to be too much for us at our home office we can sneak out for a couple of days and head up the mountains to that special place. Up there, we go to bed at night with the woodsy sounds and smells lulling us to sleep, and we are awakened refreshed in the morning by the twittering of the birds in the rosemary that grows wild on the hillside. We rise to see the sun creeping over the purple-shaded mountains, with just enough morning light to allow us to catch sight of the deer grazing in the valley below alongside the pools of water in the dappled riverbed.

Ahhh, how glorious it is to lift up our eyes unto those hills!

Yet this is not just a place for us to get away physically. No, it is also a place of spiritual refreshment. We always enjoy reading the Bible together out loud when we have time, but up in that relaxed atmosphere, we *make* the time. And what's more, we pause to reflect and meditate on what we read. We discuss it, and then we take the time to pray over it.

Our bodies grow weary with work and they need to get away to the mountains and rest. Yet while we are not so quick to recognize it, our souls also grow weary, and they, too, need to be restored. That's when it is *really* time for us to lift our eyes up to the hills. In fact, it is at those times that we are most in need of refreshment, encouragement, and restoration.

When we look up to the Source of our strength and help, our eyes become completely refocused. Our spiritual perspective is restored. Our hope is renewed. Faith and trust once again become our reality.

When we head down the mountain and back home, the telephone is still ringing in our house, the computers are still beckoning, and the piles of work that were nagging to be done have grown higher and are calling out more urgently than ever. Yet something has changed. No longer are we completely focused on them. No longer do they control our lives. Now our attention is fixed on the Lord, who made the heavens and the earth, and everything else is secondary.

Do you have a special place where you feel you can figuratively say "Here I lift my eyes up to the hills"? It doesn't have to be away—it may be a public park, or even your own garden. Either way, we encourage you to find such a place and make it your own.

Prayer:

O Father, Creator of heaven and earth, we acknowledge You as the only true source of strength for us and for our marriage. We lift up our eyes and ask Your help as we strive to make good decisions about carving out times of restoration and reflection.

ELEVEN

A Few of Her Favorite Things

I have eaten my honeycomb and my honey; I have drunk my wine and my milk.

SONG OF SOLOMON 5:1

One of the first times I took Kay to dinner, we both ordered steak. I was happily tucking into mine when I happened to glance over to see if Kay was enjoying hers as well. I saw her cut a good-sized piece out of the middle and set it on the side of her plate. *Hmmmm,* I thought, *I wonder if it's too rare for her.*

Then I saw her set a big, beautiful, plump piece of asparagus off to the side, next to her piece of steak. *Guess they served her more than she can eat,* I thought. *If she doesn't want that, I'll sure be glad to help out.*

A little bit later she took a tasty, juicy sautéed mushroom from among several on her plate and set it off to the side, to join the steak and asparagus. Now my mouth was really watering, despite all the luscious food still on my own plate.

"Are you, uh, not going to finish that?" I asked, hopefully.

"What?" she answered, puzzled. Then she laughed when she realized what I had in mind. "Oh, I'm going to eat those—I'm just saving back the best for my 'last tastes.'"

It turns out she's been doing that most of her life—saving the best for the last. Where food is concerned, she has such an exquisite sense of taste and smell that she is, in effect, an "undeclared gourmet." She doesn't think of herself that way, but she really can and does savor flavors like no one else I know. For example …

We once had a really indulgent, expensive dessert after a dinner out: a chocolate mousse torte glazed with a raspberry sauce. We shared it, and boy, was it delicious! Yet where I ate my half quickly, Kay spent at least fifteen minutes savoring and lingering over hers. And while I had coffee with mine, Kay had only water—she didn't want to "spoil" the taste of the chocolate and raspberries. Not only that, but three hours later—I am *not* exaggerating—she was still exclaiming about the taste of the dessert on her tongue.

(She is, by the way, the only person I know who can make a chocolate truffle last all day, sometimes two or three days. She nibbles on it every few hours and takes another bite only when she can no longer taste the last bite—no kidding!)

Well, this "favorite thing" idea carries over into other parts of our lives as well. After a movie she'll ask me, "What was your favorite part?" After a vacation she'll ask, "What did you enjoy most?" When we've had a fine meal she's made, she'll say, "What did you like best?"

I have to admit that it annoyed me some at first because I'm just not used to thinking in those terms. Yet the longer I've been married to her, the more I've come to love and appreciate this little idiosyncrasy. Not only that, it's created in me a greater appreciation for all those little things we have together, most especially each precious day the good Lord gives us to share. I can't express how glad I am that God led me to Kay. I've now learned how to enjoy *my* favorite things—and leading the list is Kay herself!

Prayer:
Thank You, God, that in Your infinite wisdom and kindness You joined me with someone who shows me daily how to love life and all the many little pleasures You have created as part of it.

TWELVE

Never Too Much

Give thanks to the God of heaven. His love endures forever.

Psalm 136:26

For several years Dan and I traveled throughout California, teaching writing classes at the various campuses of the California state university system. To make the most of our time, while one of us was teaching, the other would sit in the back of the room and critique the manuscripts students had submitted for our evaluation. One day, after I had been teaching all morning, I ducked back to where Dan was deeply engrossed in a neatly typed manuscript.

"Is it any good?" I whispered.

He looked up and shook his head. "Not really."

"No?" I asked. I had glanced at that particular manuscript earlier and it had appeared to be pretty well written. "What's wrong with it?"

"Hmph!" Dan snorted. "This guy is repetitive, redundant, and he says the same thing again and again!"

Pretty funny coming from Dan the editor!

Not so funny coming from the writer who wanted to be taken seriously.

According to our minister at church, when something is repeated in Scripture, it is because the Hebrew-speaking author intended that particular point to be emphasized. It is a way of verbally underlining a thought. The writer wants to make absolutely certain the reader doesn't miss what is being said.

Wow! The writer of Psalm 136 certainly had a point he didn't want us to miss. At the end of each thought—twenty-six times, to be exact—he repeats the phrase, *His [God's] love endures forever.*

That's not the only repetition, either. *Give thanks to the Lord,* we are told ... then we are told again three more times.

We are called to praise this worthy God, this Lord of all creation, this redeemer of Israel, this doer of great and miraculous acts. And again and again, at the end of each line, we are reminded that *His great love endures forever.*

When is it OK to be repetitive and redundant, and to say the same thing again and again? When you are giving a message that really must be heard! When you are giving a message of praise to the God of the universe!

In your prayer time today, why not take the time to be redundant in your praise for the Holy God who is worthy of all glory and honor and praise? Why not be repetitive in your expressions of gratitude to your Savior? Why not, with the psalmist, say again and again, *His great love endures forever?*

Prayer:

We praise You, Almighty God, for who and what You are. May we never cease to give You thanks for the mercies You shower upon us. And most of all, may we never cease to praise and thank You for Your love that endures forever.

THIRTEEN

A Mountaintop Experience

It is as if the dew of Mount Hermon were falling on Mount Zion. For the Lord bestows his blessing, even life forevermore.

PSALM 133:3

From my earliest memories all through my growing up years and throughout my adulthood, Mount Hermon Christian Conference Center has been a pivotally important part of my life. It was in that beautiful place, among the towering redwoods and sun-dappled creeks that I romped as a young child, and that I had my first boyfriend when I was a gawky thirteen-year-old. It was there, around the crackling campfire, I first talked openly of my desire to follow Jesus. As a twenty-three-year-old bride, it was one of the first places I took my new husband, and it quickly became a favorite for Larry and me. As our family grew, we spent many happy summers at family camp, building memories of our own. Mount Hermon is woven deeply into the fiber of my heart.

"Dan," I suggested early in our marriage, "let's go to a couples' conference at Mount Hermon."

Now, Dan was well aware of the wonderful memories Mount Hermon held for me—not only of my childhood, but of my former married life and my family. He knew all about the conferences Larry and I had gone to together. At the same time, I knew perfectly well that Mount Hermon meant nothing to Dan. He'd never heard of the place before he knew me. His only history there was the stories I had told him of my adventures from the past. And yet, amazingly, he agreed to go.

The conference was held on the first weekend in March, and the weather was unseasonably glorious—sunny and warm, with just the whisper of a chill in the morning and at night. The ground was decorated with blankets of daffodils and tulips in full bloom, and dancing above them in the breeze were lacy dogwood and Japanese cherry trees overflowing with blossoms. Towering over all were the majestic redwoods.

The people were friendly, the food delicious, and the speaker inspirational. In the afternoon Dan and I walked the trails I had skipped over as a child, strolled along as a young bride, hiked as a mother. I babbled nonstop, telling Dan stories about every bridge, every sandy beach, every winding trail. At the end of the hike we stopped at the fountain and stuffed ourselves with banana splits, just as I'd done in the old days.

Dan gave me a very special gift of love that weekend. He unselfishly allowed me to share with him something that was an important part of my life that had not included him. And a wonderful thing happened in return. Mount Hermon has become a wonderful part of his life, too!

Is there something your spouse would like to share with you, but you have been reluctant because it causes you to feel awkward? What might it mean if you were to make a gift to your partner by agreeing, no strings attached? What's the worst thing that could happen? What's the best?

Prayer:

We thank You, almighty God, for all the experiences that went into making each of us who and what we are. Grant us the grace to open our hearts to one another freely and completely, and the trust to accept each other.

FOURTEEN

An Eternal Gift

I have no greater joy than to hear that my children are walking in the truth.

3 JOHN 4

Dan and I had only been married a month when an editor from Servant Publications telephoned about a possible writing assignment. "We need someone to do a book for grandmothers," she said. "Since we did that wedding book with you and your daughter Lisa seven years ago, we thought you just might be the person to do this book. What do you think?"

"Nope," I answered, "I'm not a grandmother." I was a lot of things—the mother of two grown children, a widow of two years, a newlywed—but not a grandmother.

"Thanks, anyway," she said. "We'll keep you in mind for another job, but for this book we need a grandmother."

I thanked her for thinking of me and hung up the phone. When I told Dan about the conversation, he said, "Hey, what about *my* grandchildren?"

"Oh, yeah!" I replied.

How could I forget? Dan's daughter Sara and son-in-law Jim had four children, and I'd known them all since they were born. They lived less than five miles from us. We saw them all the time; in fact, I took care of them frequently. The children and I even had favorite games only we played. Yet I had never once thought of them as my grandchildren.

"Call her back," Dan said.

So I did.

"I just realized," I told the editor somewhat sheepishly, "I *do* have grandchildren. Four of them—a seven-year-old, a five-year-old, and twin two-year-olds. And I would be happy to do the book."

That's how grandmother-hood crept up on me. I joyfully discovered it as I wrote *Quiet Moments for Grandmothers*.

Dan and I don't always see eye to eye on grandparenting. I tend to baby the children more and to give in to them even when I know I shouldn't. Dan is firmer with them. And although we know full well the dangers of permitting children to "divide and conquer," we have had to learn all over again the importance of establishing our expectations and boundaries in the privacy of our room and presenting a united front to the children. Though we don't always agree in private, in front of the kids we have learned to stick together.

On one thing we are eternally united—we want to do anything and everything we can to encourage our grandchildren to know God and to walk with Him all their lives.

Prayer:

Dear Abba Father, please take our words and deeds and use them all to bring our grandchildren to Yourself. Please teach them to walk in Your truth.

FIFTEEN

Honest-Honest?

An honest answer is like a kiss on the lips.
PROVERBS 24:26

"This above all," says Polonius in Shakespeare's *Hamlet*, "to thine own self be true. And it must follow, as the night the day, thou canst not then be false to any man."

What is truth? Well, there's human truth and there's God's truth, and they are seldom the same. Human truth, like human love, tends to be conditional; God's truth is absolute, never varying. When Paul says in 1 Corinthians 13:6, "Love rejoices in the truth," he is talking about God's truth. This means when people who profess to love one another share their lives with one another, they do so with as much of God's own truth as they can humanly manage.

Yet what husband doesn't want to dive for cover when his wife asks, "Honey, do you think I've put on a little weight?"—especially if she really is carrying some extra poundage. And what wife wouldn't rather change the subject when her husband asks, "Do you think I've held up better than your high school sweetheart?" when her old flame still looks like Tom Cruise and her hubby now looks more like Elmer Fudd.

Most of us would agree that literal truth would be a bad choice here. (Remember, "love is kind," too.) A compassionate spouse would be gentle, tender, and human in answering either question. No, we human beings want God's truth only occasionally, but when we ask for it, that's what we want, with no dancing around.

So Kay and I have worked out a system: If either of us asks a "hard" question ("Do I really look like Elmer Fudd?"), the other is allowed to fudge the answer a little, as part of being tender, gentle, and compassionate ("No, Hon—more like Yul Brynner."). Then the question-asker gets to say, just once, "Honest?" And the question-answerer is allowed to say, just once, "Honest. Really." We let it go at that; we're both happy with the human version of truth.

Yet when either of us wants absolute truth—God's own truth—we change the question slightly: we add another "honest," so it becomes "honest-honest?" This means, "pull no punches, give it to me straight. I want to know everything."

Now, we wouldn't use "honest-honest" for something like a resemblance to Elmer Fudd—I already know I'm a ringer for him, so that would be silly. No, we bring it out only when there is something of momentous importance to be dealt with, which is pretty darn seldom, and even then only with great reluctance.

That's because we both know, and agree, that honest-honest means we *must* tell the complete and absolute truth as we know it. Anything less would put our very marriage in jeopardy. It would violate the prime basis we have for trusting one another—that if we ever really *had* to know, we could rely on the complete honesty of the other.

Fortunately, because of Kay's basic good character, I've never really had to worry much about using honest-honest, and I hope she feels the same about me. Still, it's nice to know we could ask, and the other would answer completely. (I'd ask her if she means like Yul Brynner in *The King and I*, or Yul Brynner in *Westworld*, but I don't want to press my luck.)

Prayer:
Holy Father, help us to know Your eternal truth, that we may be set free.

SIXTEEN

What If...?

Peter replied, "Even if all fall away on account of you, I never will."

MATTHEW 26:33

I was in India, interviewing women for an upcoming book on the poorest of the poor women who struggle to serve Christ in the areas of the earth most inhospitable to Christianity. After listening to their stories of persecution and suffering, I asked if they had any questions for me. Shyly, one of the four women sitting around me said she did.

"Did you ever go hungry because you're a Christian?" she asked through the translator.

"No," I said. "I never did."

"Did you ever have your house taken away?" asked another.

"No," I said. "No, I never did."

"Did you ever lose your job?" inquired the third.

I shifted uneasily in my seat. "No," I said.

"When people find out you are a Christian, do they throw rocks at you?"

"No. No one throws rocks."

"Has anyone ever thrown you in a fire because you are a Christian?" It was the first woman again, and she was leaning forward, eagerly awaiting my answer. I didn't have to ask the source of the scars on her own dark brown arms.

"No," I said. "In America those things don't happen. In America it's against the law to throw people out of their houses or take away their jobs or stone them or throw them in the fire because they are Christians."

The women fell silent. They just stared at me with their large black eyes. Finally one woman said earnestly, "In America, then, how do you know what it means to be a Christian if it is so easy for you?"

As I was trying to figure out how to answer her, another woman asked, "In America, if these things did happen to you, would you still be Christians?"

I told her the truth—some would and some wouldn't. Then I asked them to pray for us, that we in America would have the strength to stand up under whatever persecution should come our way.

Dan and I have talked and talked about those dear Indian women and their haunting question. How easy it would be to say with Peter, "Not us, Lord. Maybe everyone else would leave you, but not us!"

Yet then we skip over just a few chapters and read about Peter's denial of Jesus. Not once, not twice, but three times!

Thank you, Peter, for teaching us a lesson. Strength to stand for Christ does not come from ourselves. It comes from God alone.

Prayer:

Our Father in Heaven, we pray for our sisters and brothers who are suffering for Your name's sake. We pray, too, that You will give us the faith and the strength to faithfully do the job You call us to do.

SEVENTEEN

Window of Opportunity

Teach us to number our days aright, that we may gain a heart of wisdom.

PSALM 90:12

Our grandkids are at a perfect age: they love us! They love to come to our house, they love to play with us, they love to eat whatever we grow in our garden, they love to sleep in our bed, and they love to watch our videos. They think we're great fun at the zoo, at the beach, at the park, and in the swimming pool. They just love being with us. What's more, this has been going on for quite some time. It's easy to think it's because we're such really great, fun people, and that they will feel exactly the same way about us forever.

However, since both of us have been parents, we are regularly struck by twinges of reality. We well remember those teenage years. We have vivid recollections of how perfectly wonderful children can change overnight from cuddly little snugglepusses who love our company into gawky strangers who much prefer to hang out with their own kind. We know what it's like to suddenly and without warning be informed that we are impossibly boring, out of touch, and embarrassing to be seen around. And although we hate to admit it, in our heart of hearts we know that day is sure to come with our grandchildren, just as it did with our own children. One of these days they will up and outgrow us.

So when the telephone rings and a little voice says, "Hi, Grandma Kay? Papa Dan? Can we come over and play with you?"

we must drop everything and make the most of it.

Even when it's not convenient.

Even when we have way too much to do.

Even when Kay's shoulder hurts or Dan's knee is giving him trouble or we didn't get a good night's sleep and we would just like to have a day to lie around and catch up on our rest.

Even when the freezer has broken down and all the food is melting and the kitchen is a mess.

Even when we have had an especially busy week and a deadline is looming and the stack of things to be done has grown high on the kitchen table.

Even then.

Because we don't have an unlimited number of days and we know it.

Prayer:

Teach us, O Lord, the lessons we cannot learn except from You. We have no wisdom to impart to our children and grandchildren unless You give it to us—not even the wisdom to love them as we would. Grant us that wisdom in Your mercy, dear Lord, we pray.

EIGHTEEN

Wet Neck Syndrome

God understands the way to [wisdom] and he alone knows where it dwells, for he views the end of the earth and sees everything under the heavens.

JOB 28:23-24

It was our neighbor Dick who inadvertently named the Wet Neck Syndrome. In the early 1980s my first husband, Larry, and I were going through what seemed to be a never-ending string of one difficult thing after another. Then came the devastating final blow: Larry lost his job. It was to be eleven excruciating months before he was able to find another one. At one point Larry told Dick, "We've been hit with the *What Next Syndrome.*"

Dick, a doctor, looked at him quizzically. "What?" he asked. *"The Wet Neck Syndrome?* What are the symptoms?"

Since then, whenever we have experienced difficulty on top of difficulty, we have said, "The Wet Neck Syndrome has hit again!"

Well, this past year Dan and I were broadsided by the Wet Neck Syndrome. Since our house was destroyed by a fire ten years ago and carefully rebuilt, I had the naïve idea that with basic care it and everything in it would last forever. Wrong! It seems that these days appliances are built to last for just about ten years. Our troubles started with the demise of our upright freezer that was chock full of food (few things are as miserable as a freezer full of disintegrating formerly frozen food!), then moved on to the water heater, and from there to the other appliances. Then, because of extensive damage from the Southern California sun on the city-building-code-required, double-paned windows, all the windows in our house had to be replaced. Then the car needed major repairs ... and Dan ended up in the emergency room ... and I had expensive medical tests done ... and we both needed dental crowns—gold, of course ... and it went on and on and on.

"Why us?" we cried out to God. "Why are you allowing us to be forced further and further into debt?"

There was no voice from heaven answering our question, and there was no immediate letup from the Wet Neck Syndrome, either. Yet God did point us to the book of Job, and it was there that we regained our sense of perspective. All we have comes from the hand of God. We are nothing but stewards of what He graciously entrusts to us. And He has blessed us mightily. Just look at the time and the place in which God chose to place us! Just look at the home and circumstances in which He allows us to live! When we consider what has come our way from His hand, our complaints turn to thanksgiving.

The next time you are afflicted by the Wet Neck Syndrome, sit down with Job and walk through it with him. You will end up exclaiming with Job, "Blessed be the name of the Lord!"

Prayer:

Thank You for the trials and troubles that come into our lives, for without them we would never recognize the multitudes of blessings with which we live every day. Forgive us for taking Your blessings for granted, and give us grateful hearts.

NINETEEN

Comfortable as a Slipper

Abraham believed God, and it was credited to him as righteousness, and he was called God's friend.
                                                        JAMES 2:23

Last October, I saw an advertisement for some slippers that really caught my eye. They were lovely suede leather on the outside, and on the inside they were lined with lamb's wool. Just what I needed to keep my stubbornly cold feet toasty warm when I worked late into the night. And there was a bonus. They had a firm rubber sole, so I could even run out to the store in them if I wanted to. And what was more, they were on sale—one week only—for half price. What a deal! What a great Christmas present for me!

I subtly hinted to Dan by saying, "Hey, why don't you get me a pair of those for Christmas, tan, size 7? Oh, and get them before next weekend, because that's when the sale ends."

Dan got the hint. And being the wise shopper he is, he decided to have me try them on just to be sure they fit. They didn't. And when we went back to exchange them, there were none left in a half size smaller. And no more were coming in. But by then I had tried the slippers on, and I knew firsthand that they were the most wonderful, most comfortable slippers ever made. I wanted a pair!

On Friday we were on our way up the coast to visit Dan's daughter and her family four hundred miles north, and guess what Dan did at every town of any worthwhile size at all. Yep—we stopped and looked for the store that carried my slippers so we could find a pair in my size. We were almost to San Francisco before a salesperson responded to our request by handing us a box stamped *tan, size 6-1/2*. I opened it up and—Yes!—it was exactly what I wanted. I put the slippers on my feet and they were a perfect fit. The suede was snug but not too tight. The wool was warm, but not smothering. I would have worn them then and there had Dan not beckoned them back into the box. "A Christmas present," he reminded me. "I want you to be surprised when you open them."

I was surprised—at how totally attached I quickly became to those slippers. They are comfort personified. In a funny way, they remind me of Dan, and not just because he went to such pains to get them for me. It's that they are so warm and welcoming and familiar and comforting that I'm always glad to get back home to them. I always feel better when I have them on.

Dan is my lover, my companion, and my confidant. He is my partner, my advisor, and my spiritual guide. Yet most of all, Dan is my comfortable best friend, the person I can snuggle into, and with whom I can be warm and welcome and whole, regardless of what's going on around me. He is a perfect fit.

Prayer:

Father God, You called Abraham Your friend. Grant us faith, dear Lord, and credit it to us for righteousness, so that we, too, may be called Your friends.

TWENTY
Songs in the Dark

About midnight Paul and Silas were praying and singing hymns to God, and the other prisoners were listening to them.

ACTS 16:25

We have a dear friend, Patricia, who lost the use of both legs in a car accident. One time the three of us were talking about what one thing we would change about ourselves if we could—sort of an adult variation on the if-you-had-one-wish-what-would-it-be? question. We both assumed Patricia would wish the accident had never happened. Yet her "change" had nothing to do with that.

Hesitantly Kay asked, "But what about the accident?"

"Oh, that," she said. "I wouldn't change that for anything. It was because of that accident that I became a Christian."

Patricia may be in a wheelchair, but that doesn't stop her from singing praises to her Savior.

It brings to mind the story of Paul and Silas in the prison at Philippi. Stripped, beaten, flogged, their battered bodies forced agonizingly into stocks, then left in a crowded, stench-filled prison with no idea of what would happen next. And for what great crime? Nothing but preaching the gospel of Jesus Christ. Talk about having something to complain about! Talk about having a right to demand that one thing be changed!

So what did the two do? They started to sing. They sang every hymn they knew, and they didn't sing under their breath, either. No, they belted out those praise songs so loud that all the other prisoners could hear, no matter how damaged their eardrums from beatings.

God Himself heard, too. And He responded with a mighty earthquake that loosened their bonds and caused the prison doors to swing wide open. Yet instead of escaping—which would have meant certain death for the jailer who was charged with their care—Paul and Silas stayed right where they were and waited to see what God would do. What God did was use them to show the jailer and his entire family the way to Christ. And, yes, Paul and Silas were released—even escorted out of the city in the respectful manner due a rightful Roman citizen.

Reflecting on this story, author Charles Swindoll writes, "The longer I live, the more convinced I become that life is 10 percent what happens to us and 90 percent how we respond to it."

The longer we live, the more we agree with that. Our friend Patricia is a constant reminder that what one person would look upon as a great loss, another can see as eternal gain.

Is there something in your life to which you need to change your response? Ask God to help you see it through new eyes.

Prayer:

Grant us the grace and wisdom, oh God, to sing songs even in the darkest night. In the most desperate of times, we pray that You will make music where none exists.

TWENTY-ONE
To Love Again

Now to him who is able to do immeasurably more than all we ask or imagine, according to his power at work within us, to him be glory ... for ever and ever!
EPHESIANS 3:20-21

When I first married Larry, I was just twenty-two years old, but I moved forward with a confidence and assurance that belongs only to the young. I remember announcing to my new husband, "If anything ever happens to you, I want you to know I will never marry again!"

And I really meant it. I was so overtaken by love that I couldn't imagine ever being able to love another man.

I thought a lot about love in those days. It was all so romantic, the way I imagined it. My strapping, ruddy-faced descendent of hardy Viking warriors valiantly standing ready to protect me from every evil and remaining faithfully at my side forever ... I knew I was in love. I could *feel* it!

A popular song of the time lamented: "You've lost that lovin' feeling," but that song had nothing to do with us. "We won't ever let that happen to us!" we promised each other.

Back then, in my days of innocence, I thought I knew everything. In reality, however, I had no understanding of so many, many things. How could I have imagined that even then, when to all appearances Larry was so fit and strong, an insidious genetic malfunction was already beginning its relentless destruction? When Larry seemed to be growing more stubborn and careless and forgetful, how could I even imagine it could mean that something terrible was happening? Even when he started to limp, how was I to know?

It was years before the seriousness of Larry's condition was understood. After we celebrated our twenty-fifth anniversary, the decline was relentless. By the time he died, Larry could hardly walk or talk, or use his hands or arms. He was also severely affected by dementia.

By then, my youth was gone, and so was my romantic idealism. Nothing was the same, nor would it ever be again.

Imagine my amazement and joy when, as a late-in-middle-age widow, I discovered I could indeed be in love again. And—surprise of surprises and joy of joys—I could love every bit as intensely as I did when I was young.

I truly *did* love Larry. Yet I was wrong when I thought I could never love anyone else, because I surely do love Dan—fully and uniquely.

Love each other today, both with words and with deeds. Thank God for each and every day He has allotted for the two of you to be together. And trust the future to God's loving hands.

Prayer:
Dear Father God, thank You for showing us what it means to love, absolutely and in truth. Help us to rest comfortably in the assurance that our future is safe in Your loving care.

TWENTY-TWO

God's Favorites

He calls His own sheep by name and leads them out.
                                               JOHN 10:3

I have always loved lambs, and when I was a child I started collecting them. When our house burned, I lost my fair-sized lamb collection. In my speaking and my writing I referred often to my "lost lambs," and to my amazement, people from around the world responded by sending me lambs. I've gotten stuffed lambs from Scotland, from Australia, from England, from New Zealand, from Austria ... our house is bedecked with lambs!

As a lover of lambs, I am especially drawn to the scriptural references to Jesus, the Good Shepherd. I love the picture it conjures up in my mind of Him calling each member of His flock, including me: "Kay, come on, this way, now ..."

I love picturing the Good Shepherd caring so gently for that little Kay lamb ... waiting patiently for her when she stops to nibble tender greens or to lie down and rest her weary legs ... leaving all the others to go search for her when He discovers that she has wandered off yet again ... lifting her up onto His shoulder and letting her ride in a place of honor.

"Hold on a minute!" some people are quick to warn. "That sounds like you are getting mighty close to saying the Lord has favorites there among His flock. And that just isn't so!"

Well, I happen to disagree. I firmly believe the Good Shepherd does have favorites. In fact, I am one of those privileged ones.

Oh, and Dan is one, too.

Now, don't get offended. You are one as well. See, that's the great and wonderful thing about God. Every single one of His children is His favorite.

I am learning to stretch my love out to include more and more people. I already had great love for my own children. That came naturally. I have learned to reach out and pull in Dan's children and love them too. Now there are the four grandchildren. I would never have guessed I could have enough love for all of them without pulling holes in the original love I had for my own kids, but I do.

Still, I'll have to admit that I don't know how to love each person both inclusively and exclusively at the same time. However good my intentions and however determined my resolve, I cannot love unconditionally. I just don't have it in me.

Only God can do that.

In which directions are you stretching your love? Is there someone who is presenting you with a special challenge? How might you demonstrate your love to that person this week?

Prayer:

Thank You for showing me what it means to be truly loved for nothing at all except who I am. Thank You for caring for me as only the Good Shepherd can. Help me to love as I have been loved.

TWENTY-THREE

Pray First!

Is anyone among you in trouble? He should pray.
JAMES 5:3

*D*an had been sick for several days, and we just were not sure what the problem was. He does have a tendency to get dehydrated, so we keep a good supply of Gatorade on hand, and he was drinking it in quarts. Still, he wasn't looking good. I made soup and brought juice and loaded him up with water, and he swallowed potassium tablets by the handful. Yet he continued to look drawn.

As the day wore on Dan began to complain about cramps in his legs. Not a good sign. We pulled out our medical books and consulted them. They suggested more of what we were already doing, so we did more. Plus we added hot baths to ease the cramps. Oh, yes ... we stuck in a few more of those potassium tablets just for good measure. Hey, if a few were good, more would be better, right?

By evening, the cramps were worse and Dan was looking downright peaked. I called the pharmacist and he suggested a particular formula made for children who were suffering from dehydration, so I went to the drug store and bought a whole case. Dan drank and drank and drank, until he could drink no more. The cramps got worse and Dan's face began to look pale and drawn.

By the next morning, I was alarmed at the way he looked. His eyes seemed sunken, and his face was gray and wrinkled like an old man's. The cramps in his legs were so severe that he could hardly get out of bed.

"That's it!" I said. "You're going to the emergency room!"

We struggled together, and he made it out to the car. All the way to the hospital we prayed. Once there, he was put to bed and pumped full of over two liters of saline solution. And the most amazing thing happened right before my eyes. I saw Dan transformed from a wizened old man into his usual vibrant self.

Looking back on that event, we are chagrined to realize how we handled that emergency: first we did everything we could to solve the problem ourselves. When we ran out of answers, we looked to others for help. Finally, when we had exhausted all other options, we prayed. How come? Why wasn't prayer our first choice?

How about you? What is the first thing you do when you are in trouble? Do you, like us, lean on your own resources, or turn to others for help? At what point do you go to God?

What wisdom there is in the simple, straightforward instruction of the apostle James: If you're in trouble, pray!

Prayer:
Dear Father, forgive us for insisting on searching for our own answers before we ask for Yours. Give us the wisdom to understand that only You have the answers we need.

TWENTY-FOUR
Evergreen Lodge

I tell you, now is the time of God's favor, now is the day of salvation.

2 CORINTHIANS 6:11

The day had been lovely and full of activity. Now it was over and we were relaxing together in the sitting room of our rustic cabin, just us two couples. Victoria and I had known each other since childhood, and she and Bob and Larry and I had decided to come up to the mountains to a couples' conference together. It really had been a nice weekend. Now, with all the sessions over, we were sitting together, watching the glowing embers in the fireplace and contemplating.

"Let's think about what we want our lives to look like ten years from now," Victoria suggested, "then after ten years have passed we'll come back. We'll stay here in this same cabin together and see how close we've come to our dreams."

Victoria and Bob's children were teenagers, and their goals mainly focused around what they would do after their kids were grown and gone. Larry was having problems with his job, so his thoughts focused on what he would like to do after he retired. I had just started writing, and I talked about life later on when I finally had more time to pursue that.

"Ten years from now," we agreed, "in Evergreen Lodge. Just wait and see what we will have accomplished by then!"

The four of us never made it back to Evergreen Lodge. Five years after our weekend together, Bob died unexpectedly of liver failure. Two years after that, Larry died.

"How can it be?" Victoria said to me. "We made plans, good plans. It is so unfair that we never had a chance to accomplish them!"

Later that year Victoria called to tell me she had been diagnosed with an advanced case of an especially aggressive form of breast cancer. "The doctor gives me only a few months to live," she said. "Before the year is over, I will be in heaven with Bob and Larry."

The doctor was right. She was.

Fast forward to this past summer: Dan and I were sitting with our friends on the deck of their get-away condo in Seattle, talking about hopes and dreams. "Five years ... " our friend said wistfully. "Do you ever wonder where you will be by then? Or what you will be doing?"

Suddenly that evening by the glowing embers at Evergreen Lodge flashed before my eyes. Larry ... Bob ... Victoria ... so many places to go and things to do....

I had learned a wonderful lesson there that weekend at Evergreen Lodge. Dreams and plans and hopes for the future are indeed important things. Yet there is no guarantee about tomorrow. So the most important thing of all is to be rock-solid certain that the foundation stones of eternity are firmly in place today.

Prayer:

Dear Jesus, You are the Christ, the Son of the Living God. There is no other name under heaven given to men by which we must be saved.

TWENTY-FIVE

Thanks, Mom and Dad!

Listen, my son, to your father's instruction, and do not forsake your mother's teaching.

PROVERBS 1:8

When we're children, our parents can tell us anything and we accept it as fact. Dan grew up believing that cleanliness truly was next to godliness. He thought that was a quote from the Bible. To this day I am careful to always wear nice underwear just in case I happen to be in an accident. Why? Because that's what my mother cautioned me to do.

Kids don't question parents when they say, "Shut your mouth and eat your supper!" or "Just look at the dirt behind your ears!"

It isn't until we get older that we start to question. Then it begins to dawn on us: "Hey, how is my finishing my peas going to help all those starving children in China? And if I do fall out of the tree and break both my legs, how *could* I come running to you?"

That's the funny thing about getting older. Despite all our vows to the contrary, we hear some of those very same lines coming out of our mouths. Just the other day I actually said, "We shall see what we shall see." Now, what in the world does that mean? And although it pains me to admit it, I once told our grandchildren, "It looks like a tornado swept through this room!"

Yet I've noticed something else, too. Something far more wonderful. I've noticed that I have inherited other words from my parents. I have found myself whispering in our little grandson's ear,

You are my sunshine, my only sunshine
You make me happy, when skies are gray ...

It was the song my father used to sing to me when I was a little girl!

I have also found myself singing the beautiful old hymns of the church, just like my mother used to sing to me. And more and more I find myself quoting Scripture—in the old King James English—that I learned from my parents.

Not that all those old parental platitudes are gone, either. Oh, no. Some of them are still around as well. For instance, there's the one my mother used to wear out from use: "When you get to be my age, you will understand." I say it often because it really is true. Now that I have gotten to be her age, I *do* understand.

Oh, yes. And there is one more I say to my own kids: "One day you'll have children, and I hope they turn out just like you!"

I really do. And that is a compliment.

I wonder if it was when my parents said it to me.

What wonderful things have you inherited from your parents? How might you intentionally pass them along to your children, stepchildren, grandchildren, or step-grandchildren?

Prayer:

Dear Father in heaven, thank You for patiently instructing me in Your truth. Forgive me for all of the times I have refused to listen, thinking I knew best. Give me the wisdom to learn from You.

TWENTY-SIX

Good Old Days

Jesus Christ is the same yesterday and today and forever.

HEBREWS 13:8

As I recall my childhood, the rules of married life seemed quite simple. Most people got married, and they generally stayed that way—except for the movie stars we read about with shock and the handful of divorced women all our mothers gossiped about when they thought we weren't listening. All married couples had children—except the occasional one everyone felt sorry for because "God hasn't blessed them with a family." We knew married people weren't supposed to argue and fight—our own families did, but we weren't supposed to tell anyone about it. Extended families were uncomplicated—there were nothing but grandparents and aunts and uncles and cousins.

How times have changed!

Due to the soaring divorce rate, many people are getting married for the second or third time ... maybe even the fourth or fifth. And because of all the blendedness, families are becoming difficult to define. One ten-year-old girl was telling her teacher about her former stepmother's newborn son: "I know he must be some kind of a brother to me, but I just don't know what kind of brother he is."

"Wait!" we sometimes want to cry. "Can't we just stop and go back to the good old days? Can't we have happy families again that stay together and work like they are supposed to?"

The answer, of course, is no.

First of all, there is no going back. Past is past. We live in the here and now, like it or not. All we can do is make the best of it.

Second, the truth of the matter is that the good old days never were as good as they seem in our memory, or in the stories others tell. Since the beginning of time, family life has involved conflict and strife. (Remember Adam pointing his finger at "the woman you gave me, Lord" for that fruit-in-the-garden debacle? Remember Rebekah tricking her blind husband Isaac into blessing her favorite son Jacob instead of Esau? Remember Abraham trying to pass Sarah off as his sister—at great risk to her, by the way—in order to save his own skin ... not once, but *twice?*)

Yet there is an absolute to which we can cling. There is one anchoring truth against which everything else can be measured. That is Jesus Christ. He alone never changes. When we stumble in our marriages, when we face uncertainties, when we clutch in desperation for something to cling to, even then we can say with Peter, Christ's disciple, "Lord, where would we go? You alone have the words of eternal life."

Prayer:

Eternal, changeless Lord, You have the answers we seek in these restless times. You alone can be our rock and our security. Hold us firm, we pray. Only then will we be secure.

TWENTY-SEVEN

Little Things Count

Whoever can be trusted with very little can also be trusted with much, and whoever is dishonest with very little will also be dishonest with much.

LUKE 16:10

"The Bible is alive, it speaks to me. It has feet, it runs after me. It has hands, it lays hold of me." Some years ago my pastor told me this is how Martin Luther characterized his attitude toward the Bible. I have come to share that attitude.

As I have come to know God, however imperfectly, through His Word in the past few years, I've become convinced of certain absolutes. One is that God must be taken on His own terms—no fudging or editing allowed. Another is contained in the above quote from Luke: there are no "little sins." Any sin is an offense against God and cannot be rationalized, no matter how small. (I once heard Joni Eareckson Tada refer to them as "pet sins we feed under the table.")

Putting these two together, I have come to realize that if I'm to do things God's way, with no more temporizing, then all *my* pet sins have to go. Yet, I have not come to this conclusion easily, without some pain and soul-searching. It started about six years ago as I was reading my pocket Bible one day while on the road. I was having breakfast in my room, going through Luke. I came to verse ten in chapter sixteen and was impressed with its absolute tone.

Wow! Even the smallest dishonesty is a sign of a character flaw. Yet I'm basically an honest person; this doesn't apply to me.

When I'd finished reading my Bible I was ready for the news. I opened the hotel door to get my free daily newspaper, one of the hotel's perks. No paper. Nada. Zip. Hotel error or not, every doorstep had a copy except mine. Now I had only ten minutes before I had to start my seminar day. The lobby was five minutes away, and calling to ask for a delivered copy would also take too long. The only option left was to take my neighbor's copy, and let him worry about digging up a paper somewhere else.

After all, they're giving them away, so it's not like stealing, right? They cost only fifty cents ... blah, blah, blah. Having rationalized it enough, I strolled down the hall to the next door and picked up the paper there as though I had every right to it. I walked quickly back to my room, heartbeat slightly elevated, and shut the door softly behind me.

Yet I no more than got in the room before I was blindsided by a double whammy. First Luther caught me with a left hook: "The Bible speaks ... it runs after me ... it lays hold of me"—Wham! Then Luke's words from 16:10 nailed me with a right cross: "Whoever is dishonest with very little will also be dishonest with much"—Wham!

That was it. I'd had it, I was convicted. I was stealing. Fifty cents or no, it was wrong. I turned right around and padded quietly back down the hall and replaced the paper where it belonged, thinking it would serve me right if my neighbor opened the door and caught me. However, God was gracious and I was at least spared that humiliation.

I learned a lesson that day I've tried to keep before me ever since. God is very forgiving when we confess and repent, but He will tolerate no compromise. The beauty of it is, I'm finding more and more that I want to do it His way.

Prayer:
Father, we thank You for leading us to You, through Your Son and Your Word.

TWENTY-EIGHT

A Day of Trouble

The Lord is good, a stronghold in the day of trouble; and he knows those who trust in him.

NAHUM 1:7

There are times when it is so very, very good to be a couple. Times when it is terribly important not to be alone. One of those times occurred recently. A day, as the headlines on the newspapers proclaimed, that will live in infamy. It was September 11, 2001—the day terrorist suicide bombers crashed into the Twin Towers of the World Trade Center in New York City. The day that sent America into shock, and forever drew a line between the way it was before and the way it is now.

What will history write of this day? Only time will tell. Yet I can't help but be drawn back in my thoughts to another desperate time in our nation's history—the winter of 1776-77. The American Revolution was in full swing, and the patriot forces seemed unable to win a battle. General George Washington's army lay shivering on the Pennsylvania side of the Delaware River. The fighters were miserable. Starving, freezing, diseased ... they were just waiting for their enlistments to expire so they could go home. That's all they wanted to do, just go home. It was into this crisis of morale that a man by the name of Thomas Paine strode and implored the miserable colonists not to give up the fight. So eloquent were his words to them that they stir us even today:

"These are the times that try men's souls.... What we obtain too cheap, we esteem too lightly; it is dearness only that gives everything its value. Heaven knows how to put a proper price upon its goods; and it would be strange indeed if so celestial an article as Freedom should not be highly rated."

Wow! Stirring words indeed! And yet, when we really need comfort ... I mean, *really* need comfort, the two of us read together a speech that cannot be matched for soul-stirring and the giving of hope to the spirit. The orator was greater even than Thomas Paine. He, too, spoke of freedom, but of a freedom that will last for all eternity. This passage was penned by the apostle Paul in his letter to the Christians in Rome, and is quoted from Romans 8:35-39:

> *Who shall separate us from the love of Christ? Shall trouble or hardship or persecution or famine or nakedness or danger or sword? ... No, in all these things we are more than conquerors through him who loved us. For I am convinced that neither death nor life, neither angels nor demons, neither the present nor the future, nor any powers, neither height nor depth, nor anything else in all creation, will be able to separate us from the love of God that is in Christ Jesus our Lord.*

Prayer:

Thank You, Lord God, for so great a love, from which no one or nothing can ever separate us. Thank You for Your assurance that we are more than conquerors, and that throughout eternity we will be victorious.

TWENTY-NINE

Sanity File

Our mouths were filled with laughter, our tongues with songs of joy.

PSALM 126:2

When I joined the federal government back in 1969, it was to be in an intense, four-year training program that would eventually lead to an upper-management position. That's how I came to meet and work for one of the toughest and best bosses I ever knew, a man named Tom Donohue.

"Dan," he said, "you'll work harder here than you have anywhere else in your career. You'll also learn more in the next six months than you have in the past three years. To help you deal with the pressure, I want you to take this"—he handed me an empty manila folder—"and fill it a quarter-inch thick by next week."

I looked at it. It was an ordinary manila folder. On the protruding tab someone had written in heavy black marker "Sanity." I thought it was a joke.

"What am I supposed to put in it?"

"Anything that makes you laugh."

"Why?"

He looked at me as if I'd asked him if water is wet. "To help you keep your sanity," he said.

And that's how I started a sanity file, thirty years ago. I still keep one, though the original folder is long gone. At first I put only funny stuff in it—jokes, cartoons, cards, comic strips I liked. Later I added sentimental things: pictures of my family, and more serious writing like "Desiderata," "Just for Today," and "If I Could Live My Life Over."

Working for Tom, the idea was that as things got tougher and I got frustrated and stressed, I was allowed to—heck, I was *required* to—take out my sanity file and go through it until I was laughing out loud, or at least feeling better. And it always worked ... when I did it. It took only minutes to go from angry and anxious to relaxed and calm, so why I didn't use it all the time I still don't know; sometimes I was just too upset to take a break, I guess.

After I left government work, I kept that file with me, especially when I started traveling a lot, twelve years ago. Inevitably something would go wrong during the week—weather problems, canceled reservations, supplies that didn't show up, delays—you name it. At first I let these problems get to me, but then I started going through my old jokes and cards again, and there wasn't much that could bother me for long. It was all a matter of attitude.

Then an odd thing happened. I noticed one day that I was spending more time on the serious-sentimental stuff than I did on the funny stuff. By that time I'd become a Christian and had bought myself a pocket-sized Bible to read when I traveled. Shortly thereafter I started using my travel Bible a lot more than my sanity file. *Calvin and Hobbes* can always make me laugh, but nothing can give me peace like the Word of God.

I still travel with the old file, and from time to time I use it to enjoy a good chuckle and relieve tension. Yet when I want to feel *really* good, I go to my new source—the Bible. I do it almost daily, and the comfort I always find there is indescribable.

Prayer:
Lord God, words cannot describe the gratitude we hold in our hearts for the gift of Your precious Word. Whatever our need, You have provided for it there.

THIRTY

A Tongue Under Control

If anyone considers himself religious and yet does not keep a tight rein on his tongue, he deceives himself and his religion is worthless.

JAMES 1:26

Have you ever noticed how many marriage jokes and cartoons have to do with one spouse saying something that leaves the other nonplussed or embarrassed? Ever see it happen in real life when it isn't so funny?

It's really true—your tongue can be hazardous to your marriage. How hazardous, you ask? In James chapter three, we read that although the tongue is a very little member of the body, it wields mighty power. So much so that no one is able to tame it.

What you can do, however, is put a guard on it. And if you, like most of us, desire peace and happiness in your marriage, it's something that absolutely has to be done. How, you ask? Start by heeding these important warnings:

- **Say less than you think.** Make your words count.

- **Make promises sparingly.** And when you do make them, keep them at all costs.

- **Never let an opportunity pass to say a kind or encouraging word.** Make it a point to praise good work, offer congratulations, express gratitude, speak a word of encouragement.

- **Criticize seldom—and always gently.** If you absolutely must criticize, never let it be harsh, and follow it up with a positive word.

- **Speak your thankfulness.** Say, "Thank you," "I really appreciated that," and "We couldn't have done it without you."

- **Discuss without arguing.** It's a mark of love and respect to be able to disagree without being disagreeable.

- **Respect your spouse's feelings.** Never, ever make jokes at your partner's expense. If your spouse lets you know that something causes pain, don't say or do it again.

- **Express love for your spouse.** Speak of your love, not because of what your spouse does, but simply because of who he or she is. This, after all, is the love God modeled for us.

- **Let your partner hear you thank God for allowing the two of you to be together.**

Let your mouth be reserved for what is good, thankful, and encouraging. Let it be set aside for your language of love for one another and praise for your God.

Prayer:

Help me to guard my ways, O Lord, lest I sin with my tongue. May the words that I speak be sweet in my mouth and a fragrant offering to You.

THIRTY-ONE

The Gift of Forgiveness

Be kind and compassionate to one another, forgiving each other, just as in Christ God forgave you.
EPHESIANS 4:32

"Our stupidest fight was about the best way to wash the dog," said Sharon, a forty-six-year-old wife of two years. "We both got angry, and Jim ended up calling me some pretty unflattering names."

Still fuming, Sharon told her sister about it the next day. Her sister's advice was simple: "Forgive him and move on."

"Forgive him?!" Sharon exclaimed. "And just why should I be the one to go crawling over there and do the forgiving? If he wants to be forgiven, he can jolly well come crawling over here to me!"

As much as we hate to admit it, we know exactly how Sharon felt. We have been there on her side of a stupid conflict—both of us. You hate the fight. And, sure, you know in your heart of hearts that you aren't totally innocent in the entire thing, and yet ... darn it! ... you aren't the only one to blame, either! And if you apologize and ask forgiveness, or too easily forgive and let the hurts and insults go, well, aren't you getting taken advantage of here? It just isn't fair! Thinking of it that way makes you angry all over again!

Let us submit another possible line of reasoning: What would happen if you were to forgive your spouse as much as you would like to be forgiven *by* your spouse? That's right. Take a moment to think of the stupidest thing you have ever done—the most inconsiderate, the most thoughtless, the most selfish. Maybe your spouse knows about it, or maybe not. Either way, to what degree would you want to be forgiven? Graciously? With open arms? Without any reminders—either overtly or subtly—about how badly you have been acting? Without references to how many times you have done foolish things before and the enormous likelihood that you will be doing them another time? Without ultimatums about what will happen should you ever do such an idiotic thing again?

Here's something else to consider: sometimes forgiveness is actually a gift to yourself. The less you feel like forgiving, the more true this fact is. That's because forgiveness can actually release you from the pain of the offense.

No wonder forgiveness is God's way. In Colossians 4:10 we read, "Bear with each other and forgive whatever grievances you may have against one another. Forgive as the Lord forgave you."

Is there someone you need to be willing to forgive? Will you take the first step toward forgiveness today?

Prayer:

Thank You, Father God, for setting the ultimate example of forgiveness by forgiving my sins and removing them from me as far as the east is from the west.

THIRTY-TWO

Time Flies—Or Does It?

With the Lord a day is like a thousand years, and a thousand years are like a day.

2 PETER 3:8

*L*ast December, Kay and I drove the four hundred miles from Santa Barbara to Santa Rosa to see the kids for Christmas. On behalf of much of the extended family we were also bringing lots of presents to my daughter, her husband, and the four grandchildren.

It's about an eight-hour drive and we finally got there about seven that evening. After much joyous hugging and kissing, we unloaded a trunkful—literally—of presents for everybody.

As we were carrying the goodies into the house, I noticed a piece of paper taped to the wall near the front door. But instead of the usual cute little drawing that seven-year-old Sage or nine-year-old Phoenix might have done, this piece was just covered with X's—eight columns, with three X's stacked neatly in each column.

My daughter Sara laughed when she saw me staring at it and explained, "That's what I had to come up with when the kids kept asking how long it would be before you got here."

I looked at her, still puzzled, so she elaborated. "At first I just said, 'Gramma Kay and Papa Dan will be here in eight hours,' but they couldn't understand just how long that would be. So I made this little chart, breaking each hour into three twenty-minute boxes, so each column made one hour.

"Then, every time the kids asked me 'How long has it been now?'

I looked at the clock and crossed off as many boxes as had passed since the last time they asked—which was usually just one. We did that all day, for the past eight hours. I told them that when we crossed off the last one, you would be here."

"And when did you cross off the last one?"

"About ten minutes ago—they were getting pretty anxious by the time you finally pulled into the driveway."

The funny thing is, Kay does almost the same thing—she marks off each full day as it passes, using an "I Love Lucy" calendar we keep in our bedroom—but she does it for a different reason. Whereas the grandkids can't wait for eight hours to pass—time drags for them—Kay commemorates each precious twenty-four hours we have together. To us, time is flying by much too fast, and we want to savor and enjoy all the time that God has given us.

Prayer:
Lord God our Father, we thank You for all the sweet and precious time You have set aside for us to enjoy one another, to do Your will, and to further the work You have chosen for us to do.

THIRTY-THREE
Well-Aimed Prayer

I will do whatever you ask in my name, so that the Son may bring glory to the Father. You may ask me for anything in my name, and I will do it.

JOHN 14:13-14

We did it again. Before we got out of bed, we spent fifteen minutes praying together. We were pretty pleased with ourselves until we started thinking about our prayers. We must have sounded an awful lot like a couple of kids reciting their Christmas wish lists.

Oh, our requests were legitimate, all right. We really do need more work opportunities. And we do have some health problems we needed to bring before the Lord. And our kids do have needs that we had promised we would pray about. And our church—it certainly does need our prayers. And goodness knows our country is in dire need of help from above.

So what's the problem, you ask?

The problem is that we launched right into our litany of wants without spending any time worshiping, adoring, and praising God. Nor did we take time to express gratitude for all the blessings He has so graciously heaped on us. We didn't thank Him for all those answered prayers from before. How could we have neglected that? Neither was there any time left in our allotted fifteen minutes for kingdom prayers—supplication on behalf of our brothers and sisters who are struggling to live for Jesus Christ in the most difficult areas of the world and under the most challenging of circumstances.

God has promised to hear and answer our prayers. Oh, what power is ours in such a promise! Oh, what an opportunity to bring glory to our heavenly Father's name! And yet what a responsibility we have to use this power wisely.

It was clear that something had to change if we were to pray as we ought. Now in our prayer time we use this approach: We begin with a time of worship, acknowledging God's holiness and praising Him for who and what He is. Then we move to a time of thanksgiving. This is a precious time, indeed, as we review all the blessings heaped upon us and the many prayers that have been answered so graciously. Only then do we bring our needs and desires before the Lord. After that we take time to pray kingdom prayers, lifting up our sisters and brothers around the world.

You say it's impossible to get all that into fifteen minutes? You're right, it certainly is. It takes much longer than that. Isn't it wonderful?

Prayer:
Accept our prayers as an offering to You, O Holy Father.
We lift them up in Your name that they will bring
glory to You.

THIRTY-FOUR

The Sun Is Setting

In your anger do not sin: Do not let the sun go down while you're still angry, and do not give the devil a foothold.

Ephesians 4:26

There is nothing as depressing as waking up in the morning, looking over at your sweetie lying next to you in bed, and realizing, "Oh, that's right, we're still having a fight." What a way to start the day!

When we asked couples to share the best marriage advice they ever received, the most common answer was: "Don't let the sun go down upon your wrath." Only one couple, however, said they actually always, without exception, practiced that biblical wisdom. Others agreed that it sounded good, and that it was a sweet-sounding platitude one could expect to get from a parent, and that the person who passed it along almost certainly meant well. Most allowed that since it was straight from the Bible, it was surely a worthy goal. Yet, when pressed, practically everyone admitted that the fact of the matter was they just did not believe it would really work.

"If you're angry," one man explained, "you're not going to make up just because the sun is about to set. Let's face it; that just isn't reality. You're not going to get over being mad just like that."

It's true that not every disagreement can be settled in one day. Even so, you don't have to go to bed stewing with anger. You could set the disagreement aside for the night and agree to address it again after breakfast the next morning. Then you could change the subject and talk for a few minutes about the office picnic that's coming up, or the bug spray that's working so well in the garden that it looks like you will have enough tomatoes to share with the neighbors, or the big storm that's forecast for the weekend. You might go so far as to tell each other that even though you're upset and in disagreement right now, you still love each other and are glad God brought you together. Possibly, just possibly, you even will be able to bring yourselves to exchange a hug or a peck on the cheek.

Have you ever gone to bed angry? Has it interfered with your sleep? How did you feel when you awakened the next morning? Why not talk now, when you are not angry, about what you will do the next time you are in conflict and night comes. Take some time to pray together about it. Then, even though you don't feel like acting rationally, force yourselves to follow your plan.

Sometimes reconciliation will come surprisingly easily. Other times your every attempt at kind words and gestures will seem forced and insincere. Either way, if you agree to lay the disagreement to rest, both of you can go to sleep. When morning comes, you can awaken in peace and move forward to settle your conflict.

Prayer:
Dear God of peace, when it's the very hardest, remind us of our love for each other and grant us the strength to make peace.

THIRTY-FIVE

Stop My Tongue!

Before a word is on my tongue you know it completely, O Lord.

PSALM 139:4

"Oh, yeah? Well, let me tell you what I think of you! You're nothing but ..." The married couple doesn't exist who hasn't blurted out words that never should have been spoken. And if you're anything like us, the minute they leave your mouth, you would do anything to grab them and stuff them back in again. But, of course, that is impossible.

A humble "I'm so sorry" is the most we can manage.

Depending on what it is we said, that may or may not relieve the shock and sting of our words.

Have you, like me, ever wondered: *God knows all things; He knows the end from the beginning. I am God's child, and so is my spouse. We know God wants what is best for us. He knew all about those awful words and the poisonous effect they would have before I ever opened my mouth. So why didn't He shut me up and stop me from blurting them out?*

Certainly God could stop our mouths at such times. Yet by giving our tongues free rein, He allows us to see ourselves as we really are. It's a pretty shocking reality, isn't it? One we would rather not know.

Yet it is only after we see firsthand the cruel, hurtful places we harbor inside ourselves that we are ready to turn them over to God. Only then can we can ask His forgiveness and His healing. Only then can we move on and seek the forgiveness of our spouse.

This revelation of our own imperfections will do something else for us, too. In Matthew 7:3-5 Jesus said, "Why do you look at the speck of sawdust in your brother's eye and pay no attention to the plank in your own eye? How can you say to your brother, 'Let me take the speck out of your eye,' when all the time there is a plank in your own eye? You hypocrite, first take the plank out of your own eye, and then you will see clearly to remove the speck from your brother's eye."

Once I see for myself how unlovely and unkind I can be, I will be much slower to criticize my partner for his failings.

So I no longer ask God to miraculously reach down and stop my tongue. What I do ask Him for is wisdom and grace to control my own tongue. And I ask for a patient and humble spirit that will be quick to see the beam in my own eye and, if I thoughtlessly jump at the sawdust in my partner's eye instead, quick to ask his forgiveness.

Prayer:

O Lord, please root out the cruel and hurtful places that harbor words that would cause pain to those we love the most. May our love for each other reflect Your love for us.

THIRTY-SIX

A Hike in the Hills

Whether you turn to the right or to the left, your ears will hear a voice behind you, saying, "This is the way; walk in it."

ISAIAH 20:21

We are fortunate enough to have access to a wonderful wilderness area in the hills overlooking the Santa Ynez Valley. There is nothing so restorative to me as wandering out along the old trails that lead high up into the crest of the hilltops. Deer roam in distant thickets, stopping to nibble on the tender grass. Streams trickle and babble just out of sight. Wildflowers of many hues dance in the breeze over the next rise, just waiting to be discovered. I know I should stay on the trail, but all these wonders beckon to me, and I succumb to the temptation.

"I won't go far," I tell myself. "I can still see the trail. And I can get back onto it anytime I want to. It's no problem."

Yet before I leave for a hike, Dan always warns me, "Don't wander off alone. There's poison oak all over up there. And the ground is unsafe. And you know your sense of direction—you could get lost so easily!"

Yes, I do know my sense of direction. And, yes, there is poison oak everywhere and the ground is unsafe. I do know how dangerous it is to wander off a hiking trail. I truly do.

Wandering through that wilderness area makes me think of Dan and me making our way through life. Lots of things attract my attention and lure me this way and that. I have learned to hear and appreciate Dan's voice behind me, calling warnings to watch my way and stay on the path. I have also learned to listen to his misgivings. Very often there is real wisdom there.

And that's not all. More and more, I am learning to see and respect Dan as the spiritual head of our household. He is the one who is sensitive to the importance of our giving to the Lord and to others when I don't think we can afford to do so. He is the one who is sensitive to reaching out to those among us who are easily overlooked. It is Dan who takes the lead in our reading of God's Word aloud in the morning. He is a deacon in our church, and his thoughtful prayers demonstrate his servant's heart. Hearing them ministers to me.

Actually, I thank God for giving us a trail map in each other. Under God's guidance we can consult it to keep our path straight.

Prayer:
Thank You, Father, for giving us a guide in each other. Help us to be willing to listen to each other's words of warning.

THIRTY-SEVEN

No Competition

Submit to one another out of reverence for Christ.
EPHESIANS 5:21

"We are a team." When we talked with couples, that statement, or something very close to it, came up again and again. In raising a blended family, in dealing with adversity, in ministering in church, in planning for the future, couples would always say, "We are a team. We pull together."

Well, that's one of the great advantages of being a couple, isn't it? The two of you pulling together, in the same direction. Of course, that isn't always as easy as it sounds. Sometimes one member of the team decides to be the star of the show and lunges ahead, pulling harder and with fancier steps. The other is left scrambling to keep up—or ends up left in the dust, feeling less important. Or one decides to take it easy and let the other do the bulk of the work. When that happens, you can guess which one ends up feeling resentful.

In Acts 18:14-28 we read about Apollos, the great orator who was a devout follower of Christ but who didn't have the whole story on the Scriptures. He was doing his best, but as soon as husband and wife Priscilla and Aquila heard him speaking in the synagogue, they knew he needed some extra tutoring. It was a great ministry opportunity for them. Yet Aquila didn't say, "Priscilla, dear, you go home and cook dinner while I counsel Apollos here and get him straightened out." Nor did Priscilla say, "I'll handle this one, Aquila. After all, I'm the one with the greater scriptural knowledge." No, in verse twenty-six we read that *"they* invited him to their home and explained to him the way of God more adequately." They worked as a team to teach Apollos what he needed to know.

Marriage is indeed teamwork—in raising a family, in dealing with adversity, in planning for the future, in ministering in church. It is not intended to be a competition in any area. Certainly it is not meant to be a spiritual competition.

We don't know a great deal about Priscilla and Aquila, but we do know they assisted the apostle Paul greatly as he brought the gospel to the Gentiles. We also know they worked as a team, and that's the way they are forever linked in Scripture.

Teamwork in marriage has allowed Priscilla and Aquila to reach down through the centuries and touch the world for Christ as a couple.

Prayer:

Lord God, we never want to argue about our own individual rights. Instead, we want always to submit to each other out of reverence to You. We want to be a powerful team for You.

THIRTY-EIGHT
Ultimate Trust

Surely God is my salvation; I will trust and not be afraid.

ISAIAH 12:2

The first time we slept in a hotel room after we were married, Dan automatically took the side of the bed closest to the door—which just happened to be the side I usually slept on.

"Why are you sleeping on that side of the bed?" I asked.

"So that if anyone should break in, they would get me first and you would have a chance to get away," he said matter-of-factly.

Wow! I thought. *What an amazing husband! He would actually lay down his life for me!*

What a wonderful thing it is to be able to trust another person so fully. And certainly in a marriage, trust is something that you hope to build upon. As you mature and share your life together, unless one of you does something to betray the other, the trust between you becomes steadily deeper and deeper.

Yet, even the most trusting marriage relationship cannot compare with the trust we put in our Savior. At times, there is nothing to do but trust in Him. For even those we love more than life itself, the very most trustworthy people in our lives, cannot be all that we need them to be.

In the late 1800s, a woman by the name of Louisa Stead watched helplessly as her husband died trying in vain to save a drowning boy.

86 / Hand in Hand

In her desperate struggle to find an answer to that age-old question: "Why, God, why?" she wrote the words to this well-loved hymn:

> 'Tis so sweet to trust in Jesus,
> Just to take Him at His word,
> Just to rest upon His promise,
> Just to know, "Thus saith the Lord."
>
> I'm so glad I learned to trust Thee,
> Precious Jesus, Savior, Friend;
> And I know that Thou art with me,
> Wilt be with me to the end.

Is there an area in your life in which you need to trust Jesus more fully? Read Louisa Stead's words over once more, then ask God to increase your trust in His Son, your Savior.

Prayer:
Jesus, Jesus, how we trust You. How we've proved You over and over. Jesus, Jesus, precious Jesus, give us grace to trust You more.

THIRTY-NINE

All We Are and All We Have ...

See now that I myself am He! There is no god besides me. I put to death and I bring to life, I have wounded and I will heal, and no one can deliver out of my hand.

DEUTERONOMY 32:39

Not too long ago Kay and I were bemoaning our current state of affairs: more money was going out than was coming in, and our debt level was rising dangerously. Because we want to be debt-free and retired in about ten years, this was upsetting our plans. One of the debt-drivers was our house, and we were looking for a carpenter to hang some new doors. I called a friend, who'd worked on our house before, hoping he was still in the business. He was, and he agreed to come over and look at our little project the next day.

He said he wanted to do it, but he was cutting back on work.

"It's because I have to take so much time off for therapy," he told me. I thought he was referring to some sort of on-the-job injury, something to do with his back, maybe.

"I've got prostate cancer."

I was stunned. He is barely fifty years old. Then I thought, *Well, almost all men develop prostate cancer if they live long enough. He could probably have this for the rest of his life and it won't kill him.*

He must have been reading my thoughts because the next thing he said was, "It's the really aggressive kind. I'm lucky the doctor caught it when he did."

The way he said it wasn't nonchalant or with false bravado. It was just matter-of-fact, indicating that he had accepted his disease and was now doing every practical thing he could to deal with it. Even more, he knew it was in God's hands, and if the Lord chose to give him another twenty years, He would; and if not, then our friend had accepted that outcome too.

We talked a little longer about his cancer and what he was doing to treat it. This was more for Kay's sake than for his, as her father is also fighting prostate cancer. Our friend was happy to tell us whatever he could about his treatments, hoping it might help another sufferer as well.

Then he asked about Kay's recent mission trip to China and India. He was fascinated to learn more about what she'd done, where she'd been, whom she had met. Yet most of all he wanted to know what he, his family, and his church might do to help. I couldn't believe at first his calmness and perspective in light of the danger he was facing to his very life. Then, however, I realized it was one more testament to the firmness of his belief in our Lord and his commitment to do His work during whatever time he was given to do it.

After he left, Kay and I looked at each other. "Dear God," she said. "We're worried about our house and some money. He's got cancer, but he's the one with real faith. He *knows* he'll be provided for, one way or another. What an example! Let's stop our whining and just be grateful for our health and each other." Amen.

Prayer:

Lord, thank You for our friend and his faith. Thank You for reminding us that all we have and all we are comes from Your hand. Thank You for life itself.

FORTY

"And Yet ..."

Yet I will rejoice in the Lord, I will be joyful in God my Savior.

HABAKKUK 3:18

Uh oh. Just look at the way this verse starts. It says, "Yet I will ..." That means something bad almost certainly happened before we got there. It's like calling out, "Honey, I had an accident with the car, yet ..." Or, "I got a call from the hospital today, yet ..." That little word leaves you holding your breath.

Something bad had happened, all right. In the preceding verses, we learn that the fig trees hadn't budded; there were no grapes on the vines; the olive crops had failed; and there were no crops in the field, no sheep in the pens, and no cattle in the stalls. It was then that Habbakuk said, "Yet I will rejoice in the Lord!"

The two of us have just been through a time that felt a whole lot like that which Habakkuk is describing. It seemed as if everything we touched failed. We are both self-employed, so our income is affected by a number of things, including the national economy—something we can do nothing about. We watched helplessly as scheduled jobs were canceled one after another because of budget cuts. Then both of us had health issues that had to be taken care of—and paid for. Then one of our children needed help. As did our church. Then, just when we thought we couldn't take any more, the refrigerator went out. We prayed, begging God for relief. Instead, we got a letter from the IRS telling us there had been a mistake in our taxes from two years back and we owed money.

Habakkuk could not understand how God could ignore the plight of the faithful people of Judah. So he put it squarely to Him, saying, "I will stand at my watch and station myself on the ramparts; I will look to see what He will say to me."

And God answered. What He told Habakkuk was that He knew very well what He was doing, and that in His own time, everything would be set right. He ends with these words: "The Lord is in his holy temple; Let all the earth be silent before him."

That's when Habakkuk got to the "yet." When he heard God's answer, he was satisfied. What is there to say after such a majestic statement as that?

The next time you are dealing with something that is too much for you to handle, get to the "yet" just as soon as you can. Rush directly to the place where you can trust in God's timing and rejoice in the Lord.

Prayer:

Whatever comes into our lives, we rejoice in You, O Lord, for You are our God and Savior. You are in Your holy temple, and we will be silent before You.

FORTY-ONE

A Sacrifice of Love

Live a life of love, just as Christ loved us and gave himself up for us as a fragrant offering and sacrifice to God.

EPHESIANS 5:2

It was totally dark outside when the alarm clock jolted us from sleep. Both of us groaned; the clock read 4:45 A.M. It took me a minute to remember why on earth we would have set it for such an ungodly hour. Then I remembered. Dan had volunteered to drive my daughter and her husband to the airport in Los Angeles to catch an early morning flight to Canada. Talk about sacrifice! Leaving home at 5:30, it would take him two hours to get them there, just in time to turn around and fight the notorious L.A. morning commuter traffic to get back home. He would be fortunate to make the trip in five hours.

Marriage requires sacrifice. Instead of spending the day driving up to look through the cute shops in the artsy valley town with my friends, I baby-sit for Dan's daughter's children. Dan dropped his membership in an expensive club that doesn't include me. I no longer spend my summer weekends with my friend at her vacation home.

Those of you who are in blended families are no doubt finding that you are having to sacrifice much more than this—perhaps far more that you bargained for. Some of those sacrifices you are probably more than happy to make. Others you may not be all that thrilled about. You may even be complaining to your spouse about certain things that really hurt.

Have you ever considered the sacrifices you are making—willingly or not—as gifts of love? They are, you know. You are giving up those things for the good of your marriage. Your marriage, and the person you are married to, are more important than the fun times you are missing, more important than the money you are having to do without, more important than the opportunities that are passing you by.

Certainly the sacrifices we make for our loved ones can in no way be compared with the great sacrifice Jesus Christ made for us. It would be a travesty to even insinuate such a thing. And yet, as in every area of our lives, our Lord has set the example for us. We are to live a life of love, and love very often includes the gift of sacrifice.

What sacrifices has your spouse made for the good of your family? Have you expressed your appreciation? What has your attitude been about the sacrifices you have been called upon to make? What difference might it make to see them as a gift of love to your partner?

Prayer:

Lord God, our marriage requires sacrifice from both of us. We pray that You will give us grace to accept this, and to understand that sacrifice brings us closer and helps us to grow as a family. Thank You for allowing us this opportunity to make a special gift of love to one another.

FORTY-TWO

Never Too Weak to Give, Never Too Strong to Ask

For he will deliver the needy who cry out, the afflicted who have no one to help. He will take pity on the weak and the needy and save the needy from death.
                                                            PSALM 72:12

Susan and I moved to Santa Barbara in 1973, when I was twenty-nine. We met lots of new people in our first few years, most of them like us: young, starting out, eagerly building careers and families, full of optimism and hope for a bright future. It seemed back then that we were all going to live forever, that we and our children would prosper, and that no real calamities could befall us. We all thought we were leading charmed lives—that help, *real* help, was something we would never have to ask or be asked for.

Well, we were wrong. One by one, things began to happen: plans began to go wrong, relationships began to fall apart, and serious illness began to strike some of us. Mostly I heard about these problems after the fact and indirectly. We tended to keep a brave face on matters and didn't divulge our misfortunes until it was too late for others to be of any help; I guess back then we thought we could handle it all by ourselves. Wrong again.

Those who learned to give their troubles to God in prayer had something the rest were missing. Not that they had any fewer misfortunes, but their misfortunes didn't overwhelm them, nor were they embarrassed to ask for help. The tribulations of one person can inspire faith in many. Here is one of the most touching appeals for prayer I have ever received:

There is still a "nub" of a tumor hanging on. Please pray that the tumor cannot resist the radiation and that God's hand would guide the radiation machine and the hands of the radiation therapists. Please pray for a peace inside me. I am not afraid, which is a result of your prayers.

The Lord has taught me two important lessons. One, I am not the god of my family so I should not be afraid that they cannot live without me. Two, the speed at which I was living life was too fast, and I should not return to it. Please pray for me in regard to these lessons, for we know that just because the Lord teaches me does not mean I am going to remember it each day.

Your prayers make my husband cry over how much we are loved and cared for in our community. Your prayers keep my children from being overwhelmed by fear. Your prayers are the difference between life abundantly and just living through this. We cannot thank you enough.

May God bless you and hold you in His loving arms today and always.

This was several years ago, and the friend who wrote it is still cured of her cancer. Even more, she continues to be a model to those of us who, like her, are learning to put our faith in the only true and lasting reality in this world—our Lord.

Prayer:
Lord, forgive us our arrogance, pride, and inflated, self-important plans. You knew our needs and weaknesses before the Creation; give us help and strength.

FORTY-THREE

Not Distant Enough

So I made up my mind that I would not make another painful visit to you.

1 CORINTHIANS 2:1

There are some relationships that are trouble from the start. You meet someone who is much too loud ... or far too opinionated ... or downright obnoxious. You know what I mean; we've all come into contact with them. If it's just a casual meeting, you can be polite and quickly think of a reason why you have to be somewhere else, then plan it so that your paths will cross as seldom as possible.

Yet what happens if this person is a member of your family? Or of your spouse's family? Suddenly things become a whole lot more complicated.

We have a few challenges in our family. Because they are different for different people, we use various approaches in handling them. (For the sake of family harmony, I will use assumed names here.)

- Nancy is opinionated and outspoken. She does not suffer fools (or Republicans or anyone else who disagrees with her) kindly. Yet she is a sweet and loving person, and we enjoy her company. So when we are with her, we choose the topics of our conversations carefully. We do not discuss things that will cause undue friction. That way we can enjoy our time together.

- Marcia tends to be a know-it-all. Whatever we do, she did it first—and better. Yet she also is a kind person with many good qualities and many talents. When we are with her, we practice patience. So what if she always has to do us one better? We can smile and say, "How nice. Aren't you clever." It makes her feel good and it doesn't diminish us one bit.

- Uncle Francis is, to put it mildly, opinionated and self-centered. He is also abusive and thoroughly objectionable. Worst of all, he considers himself to be God's right-hand man. Our best approach with Uncle Francis is to avoid him at all costs. We are better off without him in our lives.

There are times to persevere with difficult relationships, and there are times to put a little distance between you for a while. Occasionally there are times to sever relationships. Ask God to guide you as you search for the proper approach for the difficult relationships in your life.

Prayer:

Dear God, we want to get along peaceably with everyone in our families. Give us wisdom and grace as we search for the best way to handle the difficult people.

FORTY-FOUR
The Very Last Word

Your word is a lamp to my feet and a light to my path.

PSALM 119:105

We have done some writing for a couple of different television series. To keep writers on track, producers give them what they call the series "bible" to guide the story line. This is a booklet that contains the last and final word on everything about the characters and what can and cannot go into a story. Does the main character have any sisters or brothers? You may never know from watching the show, but that information will be in the bible. What is the secondary character's middle name? Although it may never be used, you can be sure it is written down in the pages of the bible.

God's Word doesn't just show us a good way to live our lives. It tells us the ultimate way. It is the last word. It wraps itself around hearts and changes the lives of those who read it. This greatest of books, this truest of bibles, changes our thinking, our actions, and our entire perspective.

So what are you doing with this ultimate life guide that the psalmist tells us lights up our path and keeps us from stumbling? Does it sit on your shelf, gathering dust? Is it enough to simply look up familiar passages now and then? Do you read and reread your favorite portions? That's all good, but the Bible has so very much more to offer.

Here's an idea—how about reading the entire Bible through

together as a couple? Think about it: If this is the ultimate guide to life, doesn't it make sense to go through it in a systematic way, to make certain you don't miss any of the parts that just may be a very important piece of the whole? If you read it in its entirety, it will keep you from bumbling around spiritually, stumbling over theological obstacles, tripping on questions and puzzlements that others pose for you. It will keep you from trying to find your way in the reflected light cast by someone else's candle instead of making use of your own perfectly bright lamp.

"But," you may say, "I can't read the Bible through in a year, like the printed charts say I should."

No problem. Don't worry about reading it according to anyone else's time schedule. Instead, make the reading a natural part of your day. Sometimes you may want to go slowly, other times more quickly. Sometimes you may want to read only a few verses, other times you may read entire chapters. Sometimes you may have only a few minutes, other times you may have a great deal of time.

The Bible was given to you to be a guide for your life. Pray before you start and let God guide you as you read.

Prayer:
Thank You, Lord, for giving us a guidebook to this life and the next. Help us to be faithful in reading Your Word and following all that we find in it.

FORTY-FIVE

... And the Truth Will Set You Free

Then you will know the truth, and the truth will set you free.

JOHN 8:32

I don't recall if we had a Bible in our house when I was growing up. If we did, we never read from it, so I knew very little about what it had to say, except what I heard indirectly from others who read it regularly.

I was given my first Bible—my very own—on August 16, 1973. It is a King James version, plain blue, with *Daniel E. Kline* embossed in gold leaf on the front cover. It was a gift from a wonderful man named Max Perlman, who touched my life only briefly but with everlasting consequence.

I had been the acting postmaster of Fairfield, California, for the previous four months, and I was getting ready to leave for my next—and permanent—assignment.

While I was his temporary boss, I had recognized Max for his outstanding work as a postal clerk, and along with the recognition came a cash award of about $200.

I didn't know it at the time, but Max and his wife, both Christian Jews, were doing all they could to help keep their daughter in medical school. They'd already spent all they had and were praying for just this extra sum of money to meet a final, critical obligation. So to them this money was, literally, a godsend, and—at least in Max's mind—I was His instrument. In gratitude, Max gave me the most precious thing he could think of in return—a Bible.

I didn't know it then, but Max was the real instrument of God, for that Bible—and Max's vow that he would always pray for me—was a turning point in my life, what I mark as the beginning of God's calling me to Himself. It was another twenty years before I began to really read that Bible, but once I finally did, I wished I'd started sooner because then I wanted to devour it. I just couldn't get enough of His Word—I wanted to know everything it had to say, and I wanted to know it NOW! I remember that at one of our early Bible study sessions, I told my pastor that for me the Bible was like "steak to a starving man." In turn, he told me about Martin Luther's seven-hundred-year-old description of the Bible as having "arms and legs," and pursuing him. That was true for me as well.

Now, in addition to Max's gift I have several more Bibles. There's an NIV study version so I can work in it on my own, a pocket-sized one I can carry in my briefcase and read while I'm on the road, and a chronological version that stays by our bed. Maybe that's my favorite one, because it's the one Kay and I *try* to read together every morning—along with my coffee and her cocoa.

Yet the morning breakfast drinks are simply condiments to the main course—the incredibly nourishing Word of God that feeds our every need. We linger over it, savoring the lessons and the wonderful phraseology. Sometimes we get out Max's KJV, just to read again the same passages rendered in beautiful, lyrical Middle English. All the same, the truth is the truth in any version and will, as promised, set us free.

Prayer:
Dear Jesus, let us hold to Your teaching, that we may ever be Your followers.

FORTY-SIX
True Beauty

The Lord does not look at the things man looks at. Man looks at the outward appearance, but the Lord looks at the heart.

1 SAMUEL 16:7

"We beat the odds!" one woman joked as we sat in a circle getting ready to discuss getting married after the age of thirty-five.

"What do you mean?" I asked.

"Look at us," she said, gesturing to the other dozen over-thirty-five-year-old women in the circle. "Haven't you heard the old saying? A woman is more likely to get hit by lightning than to get married after the age of thirty-five! ... or maybe that's fifty. Anyway, there are a bunch of us here who are beating those odds!"

We all groaned loudly at that awful nonstatistic. Yet several allowed that there was some truth to it.

"Why do you think it's so difficult for more mature women to get married?" I asked.

"Simple," a thirty-nine-year-old said. "Youth and beauty reign."

Well, to look at any magazine or newspaper, or to turn on the television or see a movie, one would certainly think so. Plastic surgery can deal with just about any bodily fault. Every issue of every women's magazine proclaims a new diet with promises of fantastic results. Exercises promise us bodies that will look forever young and healthy and ... well ... beautiful.

But to what end?

In Ecclesiastes chapter one we read the words of the teacher of wisdom who personally knew all about having the best of what the world had to offer in terms of beauty and riches, and here is what he had to say: "Vanities of vanities, all is vanity" (KJV). It means nothing. It is like chasing after the wind.

In time—unless the body fails prematurely or the Lord returns—every one of us will grow old and wrinkled and stooped. Our joints will ache, our muscles will grow weak, our eyesight and hearing will dim, our memories will fail. All the plastic surgery and dieting and exercising in the world will not be able to stop it.

It is a wise and wonderful thing to keep our bodies in as good a shape as we possibly can. Yet it is vital that we remember it is the state of our hearts that God cares about. So what is important to Him? He tells us exactly through the prophet Micah: act justly, love mercy, and walk humbly with your God. Do those three things and you will be truly beautiful.

Prayer:
Father in heaven, make us beautiful in Your sight.
Always let us see ourselves through Your eyes.

FORTY-SEVEN

One Gripe Too Many

Now the people complained about their hardships in the hearing of the Lord, and when he heard them his anger was aroused.

NUMBERS 11:1

It's not that I didn't have a good reason to complain. I did. Several very good reasons, in fact. First of all, I was working under a tight deadline for a book (due to no fault of my own, I might say) and nothing was going my way. The people I was depending on to get me material I needed were not following through, and my calls to them were going unanswered. Then I caught a cold, which—probably because I was getting very little sleep—progressed to bronchitis and resulted in a very nasty cough. And then, as if all that weren't enough, a computer virus destroyed the hard drive on my computer. I was at the end of my endurance! So what did I do? I griped! And I whined! And I complained!

In an effort to ease my workload, Dan had been shouldering a lot of the household chores. He never minds doing his share, but doing it all was getting a bit tiresome, and what with all the grousing coming from me, and not a word of appreciation, it got to be too much for him. Finally he laid down the law: It was too bad that everything was going so poorly, but he had heard just about all he could stand. Enough was enough.

Complaints can be hard to take. Mention something once, and you will probably get a sympathetic ear. Say it another time or two and it will probably be OK. But go beyond that and you will likely have used up your partner's sympathy.

With wondrous miracles that will be celebrated down the centuries, God delivered His people from bondage in Egypt and led them toward a land He assured them flowed with milk and honey. And what did they do? They griped and whined and complained the entire way. "We miss the leeks and cucumbers we had in Egypt! How come we don't have any meat? Our feet are getting tired! We're sick of this manna stuff you give us to eat! We're scared of the people who live in that land—they look like giants to us." Instead of thanksgiving and praise, there was just griping and complaining.

Their sin of faithless disobedience, which sprang from their constant complaining, landed them in the desert, where they wandered for forty long, hot, miserable years!

I have no intention of turning my marriage into a desert of complaints. How about you? Will you join me in cutting short those whining and complaining sessions and turning them instead to times of appreciation and gratitude for all your spouse is doing to make your journey as comfortable as possible?

Prayer:

Please, dear Lord, help us to keep our complaints to a minimum. Show us instead how to appreciate the many blessings You bestow on us, and remind us to express our gratitude to each other for the kindnesses shown.

FORTY-EIGHT

Meaningless?

Light is sweet, and it pleases the eyes to see the sun. However many years a man may live, let him enjoy them all.

ECCLESIASTES 11:7-8

I've lived long enough to have lost a number of loved ones. Sadly, as I write this, another member of my family is slipping away, a victim of brain cancer. My sister-in-law Karen was diagnosed in October 1999, just as she and her husband, my brother Jim, were making plans to sell their business and retire. They spent twenty-five years building it into a powerhouse family enterprise, but the process had often meant forgoing many immediate pleasures. The idea was always, "Well, someday when we're retired ..." Yet now that "someday" is no longer an option.

Ironically, Jim gave the eulogy at my first wife's funeral, twenty years ago. I had asked him to use some references to "a time to weep and a time to laugh," not knowing then that the words were from Ecclesiastes 3. (I thought they came from "Turn, Turn, Turn" by the Turtles.) Like Karen, Susan had developed cancer, but her disease took her life in just three months, one day before she turned forty-two. We had not discussed retirement much—it was too far off. We were still right in the middle of our lives together.

Yet, like Karen and Jim, we had put off many things we could have done in favor of things "we *will* do—someday." We, too, chose to forgo simple immediate pleasures, thinking we'd have all the time in the world "later." Well, that may have been our plan, but it didn't fit God's plan. And I admit, for some time after Susan's death I was really mad at God for taking her so prematurely. More than another ten years would pass before I would begin to accept and believe in God's will, and the fact that no matter how unfair or illogical it may seem to me—or to anyone else, for that matter—it is nonetheless what He laid out before the creation of the world.

Perhaps that's why Ecclesiastes was written—to explain that success or failure, riches or poverty, long life or early death—all is meaningless without Him. Yet, it says, we cannot discern God's intention, no matter how wise we may be, nor how hard we try. We must simply accept that God is sovereign and in control of all things.

The author writes in Ecclesiastes 8:17, "No one can comprehend what goes on under the sun. Despite all his efforts to search it out, man cannot discover its meaning. Even if a wise man claims he knows, he cannot really comprehend it."

Perhaps the hardest thing for me to do since giving my life to Christ has been to set aside my human pride and kneel before Him, acknowledging in all humility that He is my Creator and Savior, and that I am lost and helpless without Him. Yet I can now accept that all I am and all I have come from Him, that I am simply a steward of what He has chosen to entrust to my care—not by my hand or will, but His. That realization gives me enormous joy and peace every day I have "under the sun."

Prayer:

Let us live always the words of Micah 6:8: "And what does the Lord require of you? To act justly and to love mercy and to walk humbly with your God."

FORTY-NINE

Lesson From a Woman on a Bus

Yet he was merciful; he forgave their iniquities.... Time after time he restrained his anger and did not stir up his full wrath.

PSALM 78:38

Years ago, while riding on a city bus with a buddy of mine, we witnessed an illustration about human nature and behavior. The bus had just picked up some riders, including a very attractive young woman. She still stands out in my memory, not because of her looks or miniskirt, but because of what happened with her stiletto-style high heels.

We started moving again and the young woman began working her way down the aisle. Suddenly the driver hit the brakes and everyone lurched forward. The young woman was knocked off balance and inadvertently drove her spike heel into the shoe of a man seated in front of her.

His face turned almost purple from pain and shock. The woman was terribly upset that she'd hurt him so badly and apologized profusely. Yet the more she apologized and expressed her concern for his injury, the more he said it was all right. "Just an accident," he murmured, brushing it off.

My friend turned to me and said, "You know, if I'd done that instead of that pretty girl, I think he would have decked me."

"I didn't know you wore high heels." (Did I mention he is a *good* friend?)

"You know what I mean," he said, exasperated. And I did, too.

Have you ever noticed that, like the man with the impaled foot, when you want to you can show more patience, more kindness, more *restraint* toward a complete stranger than you can toward a loved one? I think that man showed incredible restraint. It was an accident, yes, but pain alone seems to justify a more emotional reaction.

Yet, in incidents involving those near and dear to us, the expressed reaction is sometimes very different. For instance, I was flying home one time after a long week on the road, and I happened to be seated alongside a mother and her one-year-old son. The kid was really cute, and he was having a great time crawling around at our feet, baby bottle in hand. All of a sudden he wobbled and fell, the top came off his bottle, and some of the contents spilled on my trouser leg. No pain, no harm, and I shrugged it off.

The mother was very apologetic and offered to have my suit cleaned, which I declined. Apparently, she expected a bigger reaction and my seeming lack of concern mystified her. Yet this was a cute little kid who was just playing, and I wasn't about to make a fuss at him or at her. Plus, (1) I was going to have the suit cleaned anyway, (2) I had a spare suit, and (3) I wouldn't need it right away.

Still, *her* reaction to my calmness struck *me* as odd—until she mentioned that if the little guy had spilled milk on his *dad's* suit ... well, Dad wouldn't have taken it lightly. How sad. We have the ability to selectively control our reactions, so the goal is to exercise that control, particularly when those we love the most are involved.

Prayer:

Dear God, please give us the strength, the grace, the patience, and the kindness to restrain ourselves, especially when we feel provoked by those we love.

FIFTY
Supporting the Family

Do not take along any gold or silver or copper in your belts ... whatever town or village you enter, search for some worthy person there and stay at his house until you leave.

MATTHEW 10:9, 11

When I married Dan, he had an extra child to whom he was sending monthly support checks. No, it wasn't anything shameful that he was hiding from me. The child was Justine, a young girl in Uganda whom he had been supporting through World Vision for several years. Not only did he faithfully send her money every month, but he remembered her birthday, he sent her gifts at Christmas and at Easter, and he sent something to help out with back-to-school expenses. Along with extra family members, I also married into Justine.

Dan also married into international relations. In my trips to India and China to interview women for a book on our Christian sisters who serve God in the most difficult areas of the world, I have made some dear friends. Not only has Dan heard all their stories so many times he can repeat them word for word, but he has been pulled into their financial support just as I have been pulled into Justine's.

We do not begrudge these investments, for investments they truly are. Isn't this what Christ intended? For when He sent His disciples out, He specifically instructed them not to take along money to support themselves. They were to concentrate on their job of telling the story of Christ crucified, risen, and reigning in heaven. It was up to the faithful in the cities and towns to feed and house them. If any town refused to do that, they were to shake its dust off their feet and leave it to its fate.

God has provided lavishly for us. We have a home, food on our table, a car to drive, and more clothes in our closets than we could wear out in two lifetimes. Our pantries are loaded and our shelves are stacked with books and electronic equipment. How could we be more materially blessed?

There are many good mission organizations that need support. Most need money, but many need physical help as well. All need diligent and consistent prayer. And not all of those organizations are on the other side of the world, either. For the past two Christmases my daughter has chosen to spend the day serving meals at the Rescue Mission. Dan participates in a regular Bible study for the men there. The homeless shelter in town begs for volunteers to help with meals, something several college students from our church do regularly. They say it gives them a wonderful opportunity to talk about their relationship with Christ.

Without support, any mission project will face great difficulty. Without God, it has little purpose at all.

Prayer:

Father of all, we want to heed Your command to go to all the world and preach the gospel to all nations. Whenever and however we reach out to others, may we keep our eyes off our pocketbooks and firmly on You.

FIFTY-ONE

Someone to Depend On

For you have been my hope, O Sovereign Lord, my confidence since my youth.

PSALM 71:5

"I'm not sure I ever want to get married, Mom," my despairing son told me after his young heart had been broken. "I don't think I can ever really depend on anyone." Then, after a pause, he added, "No one except you."

That was a sweet thing for him to say, but the truth of the matter is, everyone and everything in life has the potential of letting us down just when we need it the most. I would like to say I will always be there for my son, but what if I were too ill? Or for some other reason physically unable to help him? What if he sent me a message and I never received it?

I would like to believe that Dan and I will always be there for each other, no matter what, but no person on earth can ever categorically promise such a thing. As too many of us know from personal experience, love cools, trust is betrayed, hope is lost. Parents fail children, children turn against parents, friends forget friends. Even our own bodies betray us.

Here's what I told my son: "No, you can never know for certain that another person will be totally dependable and trustworthy. In fact, it is certain that no human being will be. That requires perfection, and human beings are not perfect. When you marry, any failure on your wife's part will be especially painful to you, because your love for her will make you especially vulnerable. Yet if you build your relationship upon God, even though the person you choose to love will at times disappoint you, let you down, and cause you pain, the joy and pleasure you will get from giving her love and receiving love from her will far outweigh the pain."

Only God is eternal and never changing. Only He never, ever fails us and never, ever betrays our trust.

Have you been dwelling on people who have failed you? Perhaps even times when your spouse has let you down? Today is the perfect day to readjust your focus and look instead at the One who never has. Think about the prayers God has answered, then about the blessings He has poured out on you that you never even thought to request. Think about the circumstances in your life that just "fell together" without your ever considering the sovereign hand behind the scenes that worked out every little detail in your favor.

God has been there for you since the day you were born. Now that's something you can really depend on!

Prayer:
Great is Your faithfulness, O God our Father. In this disappointing, undependable world, we thank You for forever being by our side.

FIFTY-TWO

Who Is in Control?

He hath inclosed my ways with hewn stone, he hath made my paths crooked.

LAMENTATIONS 3:9, KJV

Every now and then we drift into a period of playing "What if?" Dan will say: "I wonder what would have happened if I had taken the job as postmaster in Ogden, Utah, twenty years ago? In fact, what if I had gone as assistant to the fellow who wanted me to work with him in New England before that? Those were some really great job opportunities back then. I would be retiring soon with a really good pension."

Then I say, "Yeah. And you know when I did that television script fifteen years ago? What if that had really gone somewhere and I had become a staff writer? I would have had to work in Los Angeles, but who knows where it might have led?"

After a while Dan will say, "I wish I hadn't sold my house. Can you imagine what it would be worth today? If we still owned that ..."

And I will say, "Did I ever tell you about the investment I almost made? This attorney promised me a guaranteed 10 percent on my money. Guaranteed! What if I had ..."

Then, usually about this point, Dan will interrupt by saying, "Wait a minute! I wouldn't want to change anything in the past. Not anything! Because God used every single incident to bring us together. We are exactly where He intends us to be. Why would I want to change a thing?" I have to agree with him.

The paths we have followed truly do seem to have been cut in stone by the sovereign hand of God in order to lead us to the place where we are now. Sometimes we long for the highways of our dreams rather than the crooked little trails along which we feel we are plodding. Many times we are frustrated because we just don't think we are making the progress we want to make. Like the lamenting prophet, we feel hemmed in on all sides.

Yet God has allowed us to travel our own particular road—be it comfortable highway or steep, rocky path that twists and winds—in order to bring us to the place where He wants us to be. He has allowed for Dan to be in Santa Barbara—not Ogden, Utah, or New England. He has allowed for me to be in Santa Barbara—not Los Angeles. And He has provided us a place to live and enough money for us to live in a way that will honor and glorify Him. What more could we ask?

We can proclaim with the prophet: "Your compassions never fail. They are new every morning; great is your faithfulness, O Lord!"

Prayer:
Thank You, O faithful and compassionate Lord,
for leading us to each other. Forgive us for complaining
about "what might have been," and cause us to be
truly grateful for "what is."

FIFTY-THREE

Generosity of Spirit

This poor widow has put in more than all the others. All these people gave their gifts out of their wealth; but she out of her poverty put in all she had to live on.

LUKE 21:3-4

As a direct result of one of America's periodic recessions, Kay's first husband, Larry, was out of work for nearly all of 1983. Up to then the Strom family had enjoyed a typically comfortable middle-class American lifestyle. They were buying a nice home, they owned two cars, they took nice family vacations every year, and they were saving adequately to send both kids to private colleges when the time came.

All that changed when the economy tanked, businesses laid off workers, and consumers cut back drastically on spending. Larry's layoff wasn't of too much concern at first. No one, including Larry and Kay, expected the recession to last very long. In any event, Larry would find another job soon and things would be fine again.

Only it didn't work out like that. The recession was severe and long lasting, and Larry had no real success in finding good, permanent work. Still, they were optimistic: tomorrow would bring a job offer for sure.

The days stretched into weeks, the weeks into months, and the months into nearly a year. During that time, as reserves disappeared, more and more "little luxuries"—such as meat—began to be replaced with simpler staples, and in smaller quantities. Zucchini and cheese, zucchini and beans, and zucchini casseroles became the principal fare, supplemented by other vegetables from a backyard garden and eggs from their four hens.

Everyone pitched in to help. Kay worked as a substitute teacher nearly full time. When he wasn't going to job interviews or sending out résumés, Larry tended the garden and the chickens. Lisa and Eric were too young to help by working, but both started buying their few items of apparel at a local thrift store. When a neighbor offered to take both of them to a grocery store to buy a treat—he had ice cream in mind for them—Eric opted for a block of cheese and Lisa got a frozen pizza for the family.

By the end of the year and Christmastime, Kay had just twenty dollars left to spend on all the things Americans tend to think of as part of traditional holiday shopping. They had so little left partly because of one other ongoing expense I haven't mentioned: the previous year, when they'd had a dependable income, they'd made a pledge to help support an overseas missionary for the then-modest sum of fifty dollars a month. And during all the months that they scraped to get by, cutting corners everywhere they could to stretch their money and their food, they never once failed to send that stipend overseas.

They were committed. They felt that much as they struggled to pay bills, the missionary was in a worse situation. Even more, they were committed to their trust in God. They read their Bible daily, especially Jeremiah 29:11 ("For I know the plans I have for you ...") and Hebrews 11:1 ("Now faith is being sure of what we hope for ...").

That's the kind of family they are, the kind of Christian Kay is. See why I love her so?

Prayer:
Father, in times of trouble and hardship give us faith to move mountains. Give us strength to go on, never doubting Your perfect plan.

FIFTY-FOUR

That They Might Be Won Over

If any of them do not believe the word, they may be won over without words ... when they see the purity and reverence of your lives.

1 PETER 3:1-2

We have certain members of our family who cause us great concern. We love them dearly, and they love us. Yet when it comes to our faith, they have less than no interest. In fact, they have out-and-out animosity.

"Are you still into that Jesus stuff?" one relative asked us the other evening while we were visiting her.

She, in particular, is certain she has life all figured out, and God doesn't fit into her philosophy in any way, shape, or form. Such concepts as a personal God who concerns Himself with the everyday well-being of mere mortals, or a Savior sent from heaven to die in order to reconcile humankind to God, or an eternity spent in heaven or in hell are ridiculous and laughable to her. A simple "Yes" seems so inadequate an answer to her question, yet she is not the least bit receptive to hearing more.

When Peter and Janet, a couple who married in their thirties, came to know the Lord, they were so concerned for their unsaved families that they went on a crusade to convert them all, but they especially focused on Janet's parents. They brought them books to read and tapes to hear and Christian music for the car. They bought them a Bible and underlined passages that warned of the wages of sin. And they talked ... and they talked ... and they talked. If the books and tapes and music didn't convert them, they were determined to talk them into the kingdom.

Finally one day, Janet's father confronted them. "Listen," he said. "We have our own church and our own beliefs. We will respect yours if you respect ours. Now, please, lay off!"

What do we do about such family members? We love them so much that we cannot bear to think of being separated from them for all eternity. Yet we know full well that words are unlikely to change their opinions. All our arguing is not going to prove God's "case."

Talking didn't work for us, and it didn't work for Peter and Janet. The fact is, arguments about Christianity very seldom end up changing people's minds and hearts. Convincing and convicting is done not by human reason but by the Holy Spirit. The best way that we can be used is by living in a Christlike way before those we love. Let them see Jesus Christ in our actions.

Prayer:
Holy Father, may we live in such a way that those who know us best will see You shining through our lives. Make us ready to speak when the time is right, and ready to live in a Christlike way every moment of every day.

FIFTY-FIVE
No Longer Children

Dear children, do not let anyone lead you astray. He who does what is right is righteous....

1 JOHN 3:7

In fully half of the couples we surveyed, one or both partners had children over the age of twenty-one. That shouldn't be a surprise. People who are more mature when they marry bring more mature children along into the marriage with them.

"I had been alone for six years after my husband died, and I was very lonely," a woman in her fifties told us. "Don and his wife and my husband and I had known each other for years, and Don lost his wife just the year after I lost my husband. The two of us had so much in common—we both liked to travel, we both enjoyed quiet nights at home reading, and we sang in the choir at church. Yet I knew I could never get married again without the consent and blessing of my two grown children. They each lived over a thousand miles away and I didn't see either of them that often, but out of respect, I needed to get their permission. Fortunately, they granted it."

Several people said something similar, and, frankly, we found it puzzling. Why would a couple of that age need to get their children's permission in order to marry? Yes, it is great to have the family's blessing. But permission?

"I didn't want to upset them," another woman explained to us. "They are worried about their inheritance."

Somewhere along the line it is important for all parents to realize that their children have become adults. The parent-child relationship upon which you have built your life for so many years is no more. You no longer have to concern yourself with every decision of your children's lives. In fact, if you try to do that, *they* will let you know that it's time that you step out of the picture! Yet don't allow that relationship to be replaced by one in which your child becomes your parent, either. As long as you are mentally and physically able to make your own decisions, let your children know that that is exactly what you intend to do.

Tell your children that you would be proud and honored to be their friend. If you have advice or a warning to impart, you can say, "Because I care about you, I have something to say that I would like you to consider. Please listen, and you can follow my advice or ignore it as you see fit." Then speak your piece and let it rest. Ask your child to do the same for you. It's what you would want from any dear friend.

Six months ago, we had an opportunity to practice this exact approach with Dan's daughter Sara and her husband. The subject was an extremely sensitive one for all of us. They listened politely to what we had to say, and we had a short discussion afterward.

Sara and Jim continued to do things their way, and we just bit our tongues. Several months later, however, Sara called and casually mentioned a change that they had made. It was exactly what we had suggested! Not another word was said about it.

Prayer:
Thank You, Father, for our children and the wonderful adults they are growing to be. Give us wisdom and discernment as we move into the next stage of our relationship.

FIFTY-SIX

Who Is My Neighbor?

"Which of these three do you think was a neighbor to the man who fell into the hands of robbers?" The expert in the law replied, "The one who had mercy on him." Jesus told him, "Go and do likewise."

LUKE 10:36-37

"I worry about them," she said. I was talking the other day with Margaret, my first mother-in-law, about her concern for her great-grandchildren's safety. "I read recently about another child being abducted right out of her own home. What's wrong with the world today? When I was a little girl, I lived in a village of four hundred people. No one worried about us kids because everybody in town looked after us. We could go anywhere and play, and we were always safe."

She was right. Her little town in rural Iowa was safe and predictable and a great place for a kid to grow up. Yet during the time she was growing up, the First World War raged in Europe. It was a "modern" war, and the weapons used created horrors and atrocities never before seen. When it ended, much of the continent was devastated; it was not a good or safe place for the millions of children living there.

I grew up thirty-five years later, enjoying life in rural Orange County, California. My childhood was much like Margaret described hers: predictable, quiet, fun, and safe. Yet I was born in 1944, just as the Second World War began to turn in the Allies' favor. Born of the inequities of the armistice in the earlier war, the second was even worse—innocents were killed by the millions, and not as combatants but simply because of who they were. It's estimated that over sixty million people died in that war, the majority of them civilians.

Do we live in good times or bad times? Is it true, as Margaret believes, that the world was a better place a century ago but has gone downhill steadily ever since? Well, history is full of examples of relative good times being replaced by times of war, turmoil, famine, or upheaval. Even the most ancient societies, like China and Egypt, strove to maintain stable, unchanging civilizations that were, above all, safe and predictable.

Yet no society, no civilization, has ever managed to build a lasting system that protected them from the dangers of a larger outside world. And so long as that world has people and children in want and fear, the fear inevitably turning to hatred, it will always be a dangerous "outside world."

The only way *any one* of us can be truly safe and secure is when *every one* of us is truly safe and secure. Jesus has told us how to do this in the prime commandment: Love the Lord your God with all your heart and soul, mind and strength; and the second like it: Love your neighbor as yourself. "All the law and the prophets hang on these two commandments," He concludes (Mt 22:40).

So long as either command goes unfulfilled, our world will continue to be a dangerous and depraved place. Yes, we can seek out safe little enclaves for ourselves and our children, and yes, *we* might be able to sustain it for an entire lifetime. Yet what of our less fortunate neighbor? Are we turning our backs on him? If so, we may be forever haunted by the closing line of John Donne's "No Man Is an Island": "Therefore send not to know for whom the bell tolls; It tolls for thee."

Prayer:
Father, let us love You above all things,
and our neighbors before *ourselves.*

FIFTY-SEVEN

The Family Flock

Yet He sets the poor on high, far from affliction, and makes their families like a flock.

PSALM 107:41, NKJV

I really like lambs. Everyone who knows me well knows that about me. Because they know that, I get a lot of lamb-themed gifts. There are lambs everywhere around our house. Our oldest grandchild, Phoenix, joins in and presents me with all kinds of lamb pictures that I hang on the refrigerator. I even have a book she made that ends with me getting both a big dish of chocolate ice cream and a woolly lamb. (Now there's something I think would make a best-seller!)

Phoenix made me a picture last Thanksgiving that is a special favorite of mine. It's a large one, with fifteen lambs of various sizes on a hillside. Some are black and some are white, and all of them have big smiles on their faces. Some are lying down among the flowers, some are eating grass, some are sipping from the brook that runs through the middle of the picture. Several of the little ones are playing together. One sheep and a little lamb are snuggled up together in the corner of the picture. Phoenix pointed to them and said, "That's us, Gramma Kay. That's you and me."

Dan's daughter and her husband and their four children used to live just a couple of miles away from us, but now they are eight hours away. It's sad, because it was so nice to have them around and to be able to gather together frequently with our own "flock." We miss that.

As our families blend and mix, as our children grow up and marry and have children of their own, as members of our extended family enter into blended families of their own, our families do indeed become more and more like a flock. As that happens, I pray that we can be like the flock in Phoenix's picture: that we can each find our own space where we can feel at home, that we can find others with whom we will feel comfortable and welcome, that we will have all the necessities of life, that everyone will be welcome regardless of size or shape or color, and that we will all have great big smiles on our faces.

Oh, yes, there is one other person in Phoenix's picture: the shepherd. May we always look to the Lord—the Great Shepherd of the sheep—to be our shepherd, for then we shall never be in need. Then we know we will always have green pastures and still waters and paths of righteousness. Then our souls will always be restored. Although we will encounter the hard places—even the valley of the shadow of death—we will fear no evil, for He will be with us. And we will know for certain that goodness and mercy will follow us all the days of our lives, and we will dwell in the house of the Lord forever.

Prayer:

Shepherd our flock, precious Lord, and bring us safely through to Your house, where we will dwell with You forever. Amen.

FIFTY-EIGHT

Faith, Hope ... and God's Limitless Mercy

Now faith is being sure of what we hope for and certain of what we do not see.

HEBREWS 11:1

It's a little hard to separate faith from hope, isn't it? One almost defines the other. Any marriage that is to last a lifetime must have a very healthy dose of both. There are bound to be times, maybe many times, when we just cannot see what the outcome of a trying situation is going to be, or how it could possibly work out for the best. Those are the times when we must especially put our faith in God, living our belief in Him every minute of every day. It is the only way we can survive in trying times, the only way a marriage can endure.

Sometimes even popular entertainment provides examples of God at work in human lives. One of my favorites is from the movie *The African Queen*. It's set in Central Africa in 1914, the First World War has begun, and staunchly British Rose Thayer (Katherine Hepburn) has commandeered a boat, the leaky old *African Queen*, owned by gin-loving Charlie Alnutt (Humphrey Bogart). Her initial purpose is to steam down a long and dangerous river to sink a German gunboat controlling the territory around the lake into which the river flows.

Yet in subtle ways God's hand is on both of them on their journey, and they are profoundly changed. Rose softens and relies more on Charlie, while he grows confident, dedicated—and sober. As they come to see the other's softer side, they even fall in love.

All goes reasonably well until they near the lake, but the closer they get to it, the more the river's mouth is clogged with fall reeds and bulrushes. With no visible current, they become lost in a morass of seemingly limitless vegetation. Finally, starved, exhausted, and sick, they lie down to die. Charlie is delirious, but before Rose collapses, she prays—not for help to sink the gunboat, but for mercy. Then she drops, spent.

Next, as the camera pulls back, we see what she and Charlie cannot: Their efforts and God's guidance have brought them within fifty yards of the lake. Yet the reeds block how close they are, so, resigned, they give up and prepare to die.

Then we see a huge storm break, far from the lake. The river soon swells with huge amounts of runoff flowing to its mouth. Hours later, the water has risen so much that the boat is floated out of its deadlock, over the reeds, and onto the lake! They awake to find themselves not only saved but at the very destination they'd struggled so long and incredibly hard to reach in the first place.

So, what's the point? First, they persevered, even when there seemed no possibility of success. Granted, they did act as though they could do the seemingly impossible on their own, but they didn't lose faith. Second, when they came up short, when they realized they simply couldn't do it on their own, they did turn to God. They asked not for help, but for mercy—and God gave them both.

Even though we may sometimes lose faith—in ourselves, in our spouses, in our marriages—we must never lose faith in God. He is always just a prayer away.

Prayer:
You tell us to knock, and the door shall be opened; seek, and we shall find; ask, and we shall be answered. Give us the humility, Lord, to heed Your bidding.

FIFTY-NINE

Saying the Hard Things

Wounds from a friend can be trusted, but an enemy multiplies kisses.

PROVERBS 27:6

Our pastor has a saying he uses over and over again: "I love you too much not to tell you the hard things." Sometimes the hard things come from the mouths of our spouses, who love us too much not to tell us what we need to be told. If you are anything like me, your first reaction is, "If you love me as much as you say you do, how could you *say* such a thing to me? Don't you care how much you hurt me?" I would so much rather have my husband demonstrate his love to me by smothering me with hugs and kisses than by devastating me by pointing out my weaknesses and failings.

Criticism is never pleasant. It is even less so when it comes from my spouse, the person whose opinion I value above all others. I want so much to please him. I want him to admire me. So I grow defensive when he points out an area in which I need to make improvements.

I am well aware of the fact that I am not perfect. In fact, that is a great understatement. I know there are huge areas in me that need changes and refinement. Often when Dan points out something I need to work on, it is an area I secretly know full well needs work. That's precisely what makes it so painful—I know he's right!

Several months ago, just two days after arriving home from a two-week trip to India and China that involved sixteen separate flights, I had to present two back-to-back workshops at a writers' conference. I was so tired and jet-lagged that I could hardly see straight. More than twice as many people showed up as were expected, and we ran out of handouts. There were not even enough chairs for everyone. And I could tell I was really dragging. Yet, after the first presentation several people came up to me and went on and on about what a wonderful job I had done. "It was just great! Perfect! Couldn't have been better! No one would ever have known you were tired!"

I didn't believe a word they said.

Then Dan took me aside. He said the presentation wasn't bad—considering. But ... then he proceeded to give me some pointers before I went on for the second time.

Which did me more good? All those kisses from the strangers? Or the hard words from my very best friend? You guessed it!

Treasure the one who loves you too much *not* to tell you what needs to be said ... and who will do it with all gentleness, kindness, and love.

Prayer:
Lord, help us to be gentle, kind, and loving when we point out each other's weaknesses. Yet help us to love each other enough to say what needs to be said.

SIXTY

The Greatest of These

And now these three remain: faith, hope and love. But the greatest of these is love.

1 CORINTHIANS 13:13

We speak of love because we are in love and we want to stay that way for as long as we both shall live. Because we have lived through struggles and tough times—through *life*—we have learned a lot. In some ways we have toughened up, but in other ways we have become far more tender and flexible. We have a long way to go, we know that for sure, and there is a whole lot we know in our heads that we still have to commit to everyday practice. Yet here is some of what we know for sure:

- **Love is patient.** You can learn and profit from every situation. Just hang in there.

- **Love is kind.** Take every opportunity to tell your spouse how much he or she means to you. Even when it takes every ounce of effort you can muster, shave off that rough edge to your voice and replace it with a kind word.

- **Love does not envy, does not boast, is not proud.** Congratulate and affirm your partner frequently with no ulterior motives in mind. Even when you know it should be you getting the accolades. Even when your talents have been overlooked once too often. No good deeds go unnoticed by the One who sees all things.

- **Love is not rude, is not self-seeking, is not easily provoked.** If you are having a crummy day, don't take it out on your spouse. Ask God to help you adjust your attitude.

- **Love keeps no record of wrongs. Love does not delight in evil but rejoices in the truth.** There is no such thing as a perfect husband or wife. You don't have one, and you aren't one. Learn to forgive and to ask forgiveness.

- **Love always protects, always trusts, always hopes, always perseveres. Love never fails.** You two have become one. Together, with God by your side, you can stand against the world and prevail.

In the end, we are told, three things remain: faith, hope, and love. Of these three, the greatest is love. Why? Perhaps the apostle Peter gives us the answer in his first letter. In 1 Peter 4:8 we read: *Above all, love each other deeply, because love covers over a multitude of sins.*

Prayer:

Dear Lord, fill our hearts with faith, hope, and love—all three. May our love and devotion be for You first and foremost. Then may Your divine love for us be the pattern after which we model our love for each other.

Visit Kay and Dan's Websites:
www.kaystrom.com • www.dankline.com • www.klinestrom.com

"Mastering Communications— in Marriage, in Work, in Relationships"

Kay Strom and Dan Kline are available to speak to your church or lay group. In addition to keynotes and talks, they can also be booked for workshops or seminars on marriage and relationships, focusing especially on later-in-life marriages.

Kay began her writing career in 1980 and now has more than thirty books to her credit. Dan became a professional speaker in 1990 and has addressed numerous Fortune 500 companies as well as many smaller groups. Since marrying in 1998, they have been working on blending their skills and careers to better serve the Lord and bring greater personal fulfillment and meaning to the lives of others.

Now partners in Kline, Strom, and Associates, Kay and Dan lead seminars and speak at retreats, conferences, and special events throughout the country. More and more of their speaking and Kay's writing reveals their growing involvement in mission work, taking them to a variety of groups, cultures, and nations around the world. Together they have spoken to well over one hundred thousand people in more than twenty countries.

To get in touch with Dan and Kay:

Phone: (805) 964-2814
Fax: (805) 967-7767
E-mail: kay@kaystrom.com or dan@dankline.com
Mail address: 3463 State Street No. 555
Santa Barbara, CA 93105